The Eight Limbs of Yoga
Pathway of Liberation

The Eight Limbs of Yoga
Pathway of Liberation

BHAVA RAM

MOTILAL BANARSIDASS PUBLISHERS
PRIVATE LIMITED • DELHI

First Indian Edition : Delhi, 2010
First published by Deep Yoga, USA
(Lotus Press, USA)

ISBN : 978-81-208-3469-9 (Cloth)
ISBN : 978-81-208-3461-3 (Paper)

MOTILAL BANARSIDASS

41 U.A. Bungalow Road, Jawahar Nagar, Delhi 110 007
8 Mahalaxmi Chamber, 22 Bhulabhai Desai Road, Mumbai 400 026
203 Royapettah High Road, Mylapore, Chennai 600 004
236, 9th Main III Block, Jayanagar, Bangalore 560 011
Sanas Plaza, 1302 Baji Rao Road, Pune 411 002
8 Camac Street, Kolkata 700 017
Ashok Rajpath, Patna 800 004
Chowk, Varanasi 221 001

Printed in India

By Jainendra Prakash Jain at Shri Jainendra Press,
A-45, Naraina, Phase-I, New Delhi 110 028
and Published by Narendra Prakash Jain for
Motilal Banarsidass Publishers Private Limited,
Bungalow Road, Delhi 110 007

To my beloved son,
Morgan (Little Shiva),
for his love, joy and grace.

~ Table of Contents ~

FOREWORD

Eighteen months ago we were, in many ways, living the American Dream. We both enjoyed successful careers in the legal profession, had a happy, secure marriage, owned our home in San Diego and were, we thought, in relatively good health. Like so many others, however, our dream included the darker elements of modern life: We were overweight, over-stressed, over-consumed and constantly in search of an easy answer to solve our problems. We had so much, and yet there was a void in our lives; a lack of balance, contentment and true happiness.

We tried many methods to fill the void: losing weight would make us happy, so we joined the gym and got a personal trainer; constantly feeling that we were spinning our wheels and wasting time was the problem, so we committed to watching less TV and working on the never-ending list of projects; easing the stresses of work by overindulging wasn't helping, so we agreed to just cut back, and to really mean it this time. We even tried a yoga class or two. In the end, however, we always seemed to end up back where we were, if not worse.

Although we hadn't followed through on our experiences, we found ourselves wanting to go back and try again. Not content with simply attending another class, we signed up for a private session at the local studio. That lesson was with Bhava, and so began our true introduction to Yoga.

One need not spend much time with Bhava to realize that

Yoga is so much more than the postures we tend to think of as "doing yoga." As we are beginning to understand, Yoga is a way of living life to our full potential, of filling the void and finding the balance we have been seeking. From appreciating the gift of every breath to realizing the extraordinary power we each have within ourselves, Bhava's guidance emphasizes the need to bring our practice up off our mats and into our lives. Perhaps more importantly, Bhava provides a context in which to apply Yoga to our modern lives.

Don't forget to breathe. Sitting in traffic, convinced that the world is conspiring to keep us from our all-important tasks, these simple words from our first Deep Yoga workshop often come to mind. Remembering to turn off the lights, the computer, the monitor, the printer, the cell phone charger and the myriad of electronic stuff we have in order to conserve where we can. Appreciating silence instead of mindlessly turning on the television or radio. Recognizing the abundance in our lives and being grateful for all that we have instead of wondering why we don't have more. Giving thanks for the food we eat and becoming mindful of what we put into our bodies. Sitting on the beach as the sun rises. Simply laughing.

These are but a few of the ways that Bhava has helped make Yoga tangible in our lives. They are simple things, really, and not what one generally thinks of as great wisdom. Done consistently and mindfully, however, they have helped us to recognize that we have the power to change ourselves. Even practiced imperfectly, the power to change is real, as are the changes we have experienced. When we step on the scale we no longer cringe and, in fact, now weigh what we did in high school. The aches and pains we had come to accept as normal are, for the most part, gone. Sleepless nights are largely a thing of the past, and we feel better physically and mentally than we have for as long as we can remember. As Bhava illustrates in this book, the challenges we face are not new or unique. Patanjali's Sutras may have been written before the advent of mass media, 24-hour news and instantaneous electronic communication, but they are as relevant today as they were 2,500 years ago. Bhava provides both a modern perspective on the Sutras and a series of practices to bring them into your everyday life. Like Yoga itself, these practices do not promise a quick fix or magic pill which will instantly make your problems go away. Rather, they are a series of tools that, if properly studied and applied, can open your heart to the power you have within yourself.

We are truly grateful for the wisdom and guidance that Bhava offers so willingly to all who seek it, and for the opportunity to be a small part of bringing this book to fruition.

Jon and Wendye Brick

INTRODUCTION

If we looked for the spiritual heart center of humankind, it most likely would be found in India. For thousands of years, long before the written word, the sages of India journeyed deep into their souls for answers to the most profound questions of existence. "Who am I?" "Why am I here?" "What is my path?" And most importantly, "What is the power behind all things in the universe and my relationship with this cosmic being?" While many other cultures have engaged in similar self-inquiry throughout the ages, it is India that has brought this spiritual quest into fullest blossom.

India's great sages spent their lives meditating in remote locations, often in caves in the towering Himalayan mountains, fully withdrawn from the distractions of the external world. As they gazed deeply within themselves, the insights and epiphanies they experienced were truly "downloaded from the universe." This profound spiritual wisdom became embodied in sound as sacred verses that were memorized, chanted repeatedly, and passed down from guru to disciple over many generations. These verses were called the *Vedas*. With the advent of the written word, the Vedas were preserved and are now the oldest sacred texts in existence. Composed in Sanskrit, and consisting of thousands of verses, they date back four to five millennia.

From this body of great spiritual wisdom arose the practice of Yoga, which means yoking or unification. It was devised as the methodology for bringing Vedic philosophy into our daily lives and actually experiencing it, because it is not what we know that is important, it is what we do with what we know. This is the process of turning knowledge into wisdom and experiencing Self-realization.

Yoga invites us to do far more than a series of postures on our sticky mats. It guides us into fully expressing ourselves with an open heart, living in harmony with Mother Nature, realizing who we truly are and ultimately experiencing liberation. Yoga teachings maintain that we are not the body, not the mind, not the ego nor the many roles we assume in life. We are incarnations of the Divine, and the light of God dwells within each and every one of us. The yogic journey involves returning home to this true nature, which is the only place where we will find lasting healing, contentment, inner peace and the true meaning of our lives.

In the West, we have come to know Yoga through the practice of *Asanas*, or yogic poses, that help strengthen, stretch and tone our bodies. Asana, however, is but one small aspect of the transformative science of Yoga. It is a beautiful practice, but if we embrace these poses alone we miss what Yoga as a whole is intended to do – to transform our consciousness from the ego to the eternal, shift our awareness from the external to the internal, and allow us to live as liberated beings in full harmony with nature and unified with the Divine.

One of the greatest ancient texts of Yoga is the *Yoga Sutras of Patanjali.* Patanjali was a sage who lived in the 2nd Century BC, in what is now Pakistan. His city of Takshashila, which has long since crumbled to dust, is said to have been at the center of global culture and an information highway of the times. Many enlightened people flocked to this thriving metropolis, which also was home to a great university where Patanjali is said to have been in residence.

By Patanjali's time, the Hindu deity *Krishna* was ancient history and the *Buddha* had come and gone a few centuries before. The Vedas and their archaic mantras had long fallen into obscurity, but many new teachings had come out of them through the *Upanishads* and *Bhagavad-Gita*, of which Yoga was perhaps the crown jewel. Patanjali sought to render the teachings of Yoga in a few clear and concise axioms and so developed the Yoga Sutras. Though there were already many important teachings on Yoga going back many centuries, Patanjali so well crafted his Sutras that over time they became the prime textbook of Yoga.

The Sanskrit word *sutra* informs the English word "suture" and literally means a thread or a line. The Sutras are like sutures or threads, composed as terse aphorisms designed to stitch together the wisdom of Yoga. Over the centuries, great sages and gurus have expounded on these aphorisms in various commentaries, articulating and expanding the philosophical wisdom and pragmatic practices of what is known as *Raja Yoga* – the Royal Path.

There is much about Patanjali that remains unclear, as there is little detail about his life in recorded literature. He is traditionally regarded as an incarnation of the serpent god Ananta, the serpent upon which the Supreme Soul Lord Vishnu lies, and the name Patanjali itself also means a type of snake. He was also known as a master of the Sanskrit language and of *Ayurveda* – the medical system and sister science of Yoga – and wrote commentaries on important books in these fields.

The exact history of Patanjali is not important, however, as he is but one of the many teachers in the greater Yoga tradition. It is his legacy of teachings that is the treasure. The Sutras have lasted throughout the ages, providing generations of seekers a roadmap for the journey of Yoga. No matter how many times one reads this sacred text new insights arise, and devoted students find a deeper wisdom that seemed to elude them upon prior readings. This is because the more we practice and seek to truly live Yoga, the more our own inner wisdom is cultivated. Thus our ability to see more and more deeply into the Sutras is brought to light.

The Sutras are divided into four *padas*, or segments. The first is *Samadhi Pada*, the state of absorption or inner awareness that arises when one finally stills the mind, opens the heart and reunites with the Divine. Segment two, *Sadhana Pada*, is on practices of Yoga. Segment three, *Vibhuti Pada*, articulates the special powers that arise from yogic practice, and finally *Kaivalya Pada* deals with spiritual liberation. I do not claim to be a sage, nor is this book intended as another commentary on the Sutras. My focus is on the centerpiece of Patanjali's work known as *Ashtanga*, the Eight Limbs of Yoga.

The Ashtanga system is articulated in the Sadhana Pada. This is not to be confused with the system of yogic postures called Ashtanga that is currently popular in the West. While its name was borrowed from the Sutras, its primary focus is upon a powerful series of poses designed to strengthen, stretch and purify the body. Patanjali's Ashtanga system, on the other hand, provides a blueprint for living a conscious life, engendering personal transformation and ultimately experiencing Self-realization.

It is not the only system in Yoga. There are many different pathways and techniques in this sacred science. The limbs do, however, give us great guidance and insight into the heart of yogic practice and philosophy, while offering us the opportunity to grow, heal and thrive. They are synergistic, and as we weave them into our lives there arises a tapestry of spiritual awakening.

Most of us live with great stress. The pace of our lives is hectic and filled with pressure. Mass media controls much of our thoughts and manipulates our culture. Physical and mental toxins pervade our atmosphere. We often feel disconnected from our deeper selves and lasting happiness or satisfaction is elusive. In short, we are trapped in a bubble of negative social conditioning in which the majority of us spend our entire lives, usually convinced that this artificial and illusory reality is authentic and inescapable. Extracting ourselves from this bubble is *Moksha*, or liberation. Patanjali's Ashtanga provides a proven and time-tested pathway for this self-extraction, like a prescription from the Divine for what ails us in body, mind and soul.

Yoga, in all of its fullness, brought me back from the brink of death and guided me into self-healing from terminal cancer and the crippling pain of a broken back and failed surgery. It brought me into contact with my deeper and true self, changed my understanding of life and opened my heart to the fullness of existence. My gratitude to this sacred path is profound, and my commitment to sharing its beauty in whatever way I am able is complete.

In exploring the Eight Limbs of Yoga, my intention is to delve into how relevant this ancient system is for our modern times, and to provide observations and – most importantly – practices to help you embody, live and benefit from this wisdom. I offer my observations with great humility and I bow to all the ancient sages, to Sri Patanjali for his gift to humankind, and to my teacher, Vamadeva Shastri, for his guidance and endless wisdom.

May Yoga fill your heart and guide you into embracing the Sacred Being that you truly are!

Blessings & Peace,
Bhava Ram

Through the Eight Limbs of Yoga
we extract ourselves from
the bubble of social conditioning and live as
liberated beings.
We find our authentic voice,
discover our true calling
and manifest our greatest Self.

CHAPTER ONE
Ashtanga: The Eight Limbs of Yoga

There is a place in the center of your chest, right behind your breastbone, that glows like a radiant candle flame. Embodied in this light is a profound intelligence and an innate power for healing and personal growth. It is in this "heart center," the very light of our spirit, where we find our truth and connect with the Eternal and the Divine. It is here, in this sacred space, that we hear the voice of our Soul, find our inherent wisdom and experience the grace of Yoga.

Yet most of us feel little or no connection with our inner light. We live largely in our minds, immersed in a never-ending flood of inner chatter. We are deluged with incessant thoughts of the past, projections about the future, hypothetical scenarios, aversions, attractions and self-centered dramas. Mass media has drowned our consciousness with commercial messages designed to control our thought process and lifestyles, molding us into highly addicted consumers of products and services of questionable value. We are left anxious, unhappy, fearful, angry and often deranged.

It is little wonder that millions of us are on anti-depressants and otherwise medicated, over-consume food and alcohol, and have a host of addictions that range from staring at the television for hours each day to thrill seeking and drug abuse. All of these toxic behaviors are means of escaping from our anxiety, of running away from ourselves. We are trying to cope with something most of us do not understand and have never been taught: that true and lasting contentment and satisfaction can never be obtained through external pursuits, that we will only find this peace within ourselves when we begin to master our minds.

In his typically terse and precise way, Patanjali addresses this situation at the very beginning of the Yoga Sutras, long before articulating the eight-limbed system of Raja Yoga:

Sutra 1.2 *Yogas Citta Vritti Nirodhah.*

"Yoga is stilling the fluctuations of the mind."

Sutra 1.3 *Tada Drastuh Svarupe Vasthanam.*

"Then one abides in their own true nature."

Still the mind and merge into our true nature, which is oneness with the Divine. This, Patanjali tells us, is a state of consciousness at the highest spiritual level, the true state of Yoga. It is here that we find the real meaning of life, come to understand who we truly are, and enter into a state of lasting contentment and peace. It is moving from the fluctuations of the egocentric mind to the stillness of the heart and the eternity of the soul.

But while the concept may be simple, concise and to the point, learning to still our minds on a sustained basis for more that a few brief moments is profoundly challenging. Apparently, it was a difficult task thousands of years ago during Patanjali's time, or he would not have had to bring it up, and that was before radio, television, telephones, computers and mass media existed! In our modern age, with all of the distractions and sensory inputs bombarding us every day, the idea of stilling the mind seems all but impossible.

We have come to accept the brain as being the container of the mind, and the external mind as who we actually are. Western culture, focused on the rational, logical and empirical, is largely ego driven. Individuality and self-centeredness prevail. We are conditioned to see ourselves as the central actor in our own personal movie, convinced it is all about us. We seek fame, wealth, success and material objects as our barometers of how great a star we are. We studiously avoid all aspects of life to which we have developed aversions. When the plot of our movie takes an unexpected turn that we dislike, we get agitated, anxious and stressed-out.

Yoga has long held that there is a much deeper mind in the heart and that it reflects the mind of the Divine. Modern science has only recently come to some awareness of this, discovering neural, or brain cells, in the heart. Unless we learn to live from the heart, we are doomed to the illusory world of duality where our ego-driven mind holds sway. This, Yoga teaches us, is the cause of all suffering.

Just as an acorn possesses all the intelligence needed to create the mighty oak tree, each one of us embodies this eternal consciousness from which we have been largely disenfranchised. The very essence of this consciousness is love, peace, compassion and contentment. Returning to our hearts brings us into this sacred essence of awareness where serenity reigns. But as long as we remain driven by the ego-based mind and our five senses, we remain largely out of touch with our hearts.

Stilling the mind and abiding permanently in our true nature is not going to happen overnight. It is the ultimate attainment, the state we enter when we finally reach the mountaintop. Those who get there on a permanent basis become our gurus, saints and sages. For the rest of us mere mortals it is enough in this lifetime to connect more deeply with our true selves and live our lives in greater balance and harmony, with a deeper awareness and elevated consciousness.

I imagine Patanjali knew this was true in his times as well, which he why he codified a host of spiritual, ethical, mental and physical practices to enrich our lives, help us heal and move us along on our journey. This is Ashtanga, the Eight Limbs of Yoga.

Ashtanga – The Eight Limbs

1. *Yamas:* (Moral Precepts)

Ahimsa:	Non-violence
Satya:	Truthfulness
Asteya:	Non-Stealing
Bramacharya:	Continence, abstention
Aparigraha:	Non-possessiveness

2. *Niyamas:* (Personal Observances)

Saucha:	Purity
Santosha:	Contentment
Tapas:	Austerity
Svadhyaya:	Spiritual studies
Ishvara Pranidhana:	Constant devotion to God

3. *Asana:* (Postures)

4. *Pranayama:* (Control of Life Force)

5. *Pratyahara:* (Withdrawal of the Senses)

6. *Dharana:* (Concentration)

7. *Dhyana:* (Meditation)

8. *Samadhi:* (Absorption)

The first two limbs, Yamas and Niyamas, involve moral precepts and personal observances that we will explore in-depth along with the other limbs in coming chapters. We can find these principles, in one form or another, in most major religions and spiritual practices. It is a law of the universe that in order to have harmony in our lives we must seek to engage in right actions and be in harmony with the world around us.

At first blush, the precepts of the Yamas might seem a bit naive. Surely, we all know not to be violent, lie or steal. But far beyond the obvious aspects of each moral precept we find a profound complexity and richness. Most modern cultures have forgotten, or chosen to ignore, the subtleties of these universal precepts. As a result, there is unnecessary conflict, confusion and suffering, because without this moral foundation we are adrift. It's not likely that we will master each of these precepts right from the start, especially given the underlying imbalances around us. But contemplating and doing our best to embrace and live them raises our consciousness and helps to make us better citizens of the world.

The personal observances of the Niyamas begin to articulate the uniqueness and thoroughness of yogic practice. It is here where we are reminded that we must take personal responsibility for our lives. No one else is going to climb the mountain for us. We must place one foot in front of the other and make the journey ourselves, relishing the stunning vistas along the way and accepting the hardships of the ascent.

The limbs of Asana and Pranayama are the postures and breath-work that most of us are familiar with from Yoga classes. Like the moral precepts and personal observances of Yoga, these practices have a range of effects from the gross to the subtle. While physical in nature, they are an integral part of the journey into Self-realization and, if properly approached, have a great impact upon our minds, our hearts and our souls.

The first four limbs together comprise the "outer limbs" of the Ashtanga system. They serve to build the proper foundation for the deeper work that is yet to come. The fifth limb, Pratyahara, is the passageway from the outer to the inner limbs and, as we will see, comprises perhaps the most important and essential element of yogic practice for our current times. Here we withdraw from the noise of the external world and turn inward. This guides us to the final three, or "inner limbs" of Dharana, Dhyana and Samadhi, which are concentration, meditation and absorption.

This ultimate absorption of the final limb is what Patanjali was talking about at the beginning of the Sutras. The mind is finally still and we have become one with our true selves. We are home in the heart at last and experiencing *Satchitananda:* Being, Consciousness and Bliss. Isn't this what we all want, to live life blissfully with contentment and inner peace, without the underlying anxiety, fear and anger that permeate our culture and cause us so much distress?

Modern society leads us to believe that we can have this happiness once we attain a certain status, fame, level of income, circle of friends, life partner, larger bank accounts or bigger homes and cars. As we all know, it never works. Stories of the misery of the rich and famous are legion throughout all history. No matter what we achieve, acquire and accumulate we are still left with our suffering. This prompts us to chase the next desire, convincing or actually deluding ourselves that this time it will work and we will be whole. Most of us live our lives in this toxic cycle of desire, acquisition and disappointment. It is at the root of most of the mental and physical illness that plague modern life.

Imagine truly letting go of anger, fear, frustration, judgment and self-doubt. Imagine being healthy and balanced in body and mind, living fully in the present moment with clarity and grace. Imagine meeting the challenges of life with steadiness, courage and skill. Imagine releasing desire and truly having contentment and peace, with no more chasing the false hopes of external fulfillment. This is what Yoga offers you, and the Eight Limbs provide a structure for understanding and implementing the changes necessary to end your suffering and become a *Jivanmukti,* a liberated being. In this context, Yoga is a peaceful revolution, a call to extract ourselves from a dysfunctional and imbalanced paradigm and live in greater harmony, integrity and authenticity.

If the limbs look formidable to you, it's because they are. The good news is that we aren't required to master each one before moving to the next. If this were the case, most of us would be stuck right at the very beginning. One of the very first Yamas is Satya, or truthfulness. Learning to be fully honest with others, and more importantly, to be fully honest with ourselves, can be a lifetime pursuit in and of itself. If we had to wait in line before mastering this aspect of Yoga, it would be a line that would circle the globe. Instead, we can begin by acknowledging where we are in our journey and seeking to embrace and embody as much of each limb as possible, mastering what we are able and moving forward as best we can.

Most of us enter this journey because we are suffering. It might be chronic pain or disease, anxiety or depression, or perhaps a feeling of general dissatisfaction with who we are and the way in which our lives are unfolding. For others it is a deep longing for greater meaning and a connection with Spirit. All such suffering is a message from the Divine, a call to change our lives and find a deeper greatness within ourselves. Suffering, violence and oppression have resulted in some of the greatest teachers and moral leaders of our times. The racism in South Africa brought Nelson Mandela to the fore and in America, Martin Luther King. The oppression of Tibet brought global awareness of the Dalai Lama, in Vietnam the great Buddhist leader Thich Nhat Hanh arose as a result of the Vietnam War, and in India, the British occupation brought us Mahatma Gandhi.

Whatever it might be that has brought you to Yoga, I invite you to see it as a great blessing and a catalyst for sustaining the devotion and effort necessary for this journey. All suffering and emptiness is a sign of imbalance, a beckoning of the heart to come home to our true self, an invitation into the sacred realm of Yoga. The Eight Limbs offer a passageway into this sacred realm and provide a lifelong path that offers us health, happiness, contentment and meaning. I invite you to take this sacred journey in whatever capacity you are able, and to truly experience the remarkable being that you are.

Non-violence
is the central principle of Yoga.
When we no longer harm ourselves,
our fellow beings
or Mother Earth,
peace blossoms forth like a radiant flower
unfolding to the morning sun.

CHAPTER TWO
Ahimsa

According to the yogic view, periods of history called *Yugas* are said to extend for many thousands of years and run cyclically through time. The great Indian spiritual epic, *Mahabharata*, composed some two thousand years ago, describes an ancient Yuga during which there was perpetual peace and equanimity. Humankind lived without hatred, vanity, greed or evil thought. People were spiritually aware, connected with nature and in harmony with all things. While conventional historians have long viewed this as fanciful, archeologists have begun to uncover convincing evidence of such ancient civilizations in the Indus Valley.

Unfortunately, we are currently in *Kali Yuga*, an age of vice and violence that began more than five thousand years ago. In this age, our connection with the Divine is lost and wars become commonplace and acceptable. The Mahabharata noted this dark age would bring widespread greed, animosity and lust. It speaks of humankind embracing false sciences, the rise of corrupt and deceitful leaders, the loss of authenticity and integrity, and the pervasiveness of violence and conflict.

The teachings of the Eight Limbs of Yoga arose with Kali Yuga in mind. Hence, the most important moral precept of the limbs, *Ahimsa*, asks that we hold a vision of world peace and that we seek to embody this vision within ourselves. We are asked to hold the light of Ahimsa during the darkness of these times, and to be individual beacons of peace even if true world peace remains illusive throughout our lifetime. With six billion people on the planet and conflict pervasive around the world, this might seem a futile gesture, but even the smallest of shifts can carry great significance and have far-reaching effects.

As the first of the Yamas, or moral precepts, Ahimsa is at the very heart of Yoga - a centerpiece of yogic philosophy, lifestyle and practice. While Sanskrit terms often have a variety of definitions and complexities beyond the English language, Ahimsa is most often defined as non-harming or non-violence. At its base, Ahimsa means not killing, much like the Sixth Commandment of the Old Testament. In Yoga, it also means never engaging in any form of aggression or violence towards others, towards ourselves, or towards Mother Earth in all of her manifestations. Violence, even in its most subtle forms, is the very vibration, or essence, of imbalance and it lies at the root of our suffering.

Patanjali addresses Ahimsa in this way:

Sutra 2.35 *Ahimsa Pratisthayam Tat Samnidhau.*

"In the presence of one firmly established in non-violence, all hostilities cease."

Patanjali is telling us that the more we embrace non-violence, the more we emit the harmonious vibrations of a peaceful presence. This tends to affect everyone and everything around us. A dog is more likely to bite someone if it feels fear or anger in that person's presence. If it feels peace there is no perceived threat, and the animal is more likely to approach the person and lick their hand or seek to be patted on the head. We all have this same intuitive sense and tend

to be instantly on our guard in the presence of agitated people and soothed in the presence of the peaceful. We all know,
too, that when we act aggressively or angrily towards another
we are likely to receive the same response, and thus a cycle of
negativity begins which is also a subtle form of violence.

The opposite holds true as well. The more we cultivate peace
within ourselves the more we help to spread peace in the world.
We cannot have this peace if we are engaged in harming. Even
subtle levels of violence commonly accepted in society, such as
harsh language and harmful gossip, contribute to disharmony
and suffering. They have the power to deeply influence the
collective mind and set the stage for greater conflict. Cultivating subtle levels of non-harming and peace carries a profound
power as well, a power that can change the world.

The greatest example of the power of Ahimsa that we have
in our modern era is Mahatma Gandhi. Gandhi was the central
political and spiritual leader of India's independence movement
from British rule in the 20th Century. At the time, Great Britain
was the superpower of the world and had colonized India with
cruelty, exploitation and domination. In opposition to this,
Gandhi pioneered what he called *Satyagraha*, the resistance
of tyranny through mass civil disobedience founded upon
Ahimsa. He and his followers, who eventually numbered in
the millions, were willing to suffer imprisonment and physical
brutality, even death, without ever seeking to retaliate.

Although a British-educated lawyer, Gandhi was a yogi
and devoted student of the Bhagavad-Gita, one of the most
sacred texts of Indian spirituality, contained in 18 chapters as
the centerpiece of the epic Mahabharata. The Gita provides
much of the wisdom found later in the Sutras and articulates much of the path of Yoga. It focuses upon standing in

one's truth and doing what must be done with both courage and detachment. Through standing in the Yoga of his total commitment to non-violent resistance, Gandhi led India to independence and inspired movements for freedom and civil rights around the world. Gandhi taught that peace is not something that we simply hold dearly in our minds, it is something that must be embodied in our actions. He urged each of us to be the change that we seek in the world, knowing that to change the world we must first change ourselves. Violence begets violence, as we have witnessed repeatedly throughout history. Likewise, as Gandhi both knew and demonstrated, peace begets peace.

One of Gandhi's most remarkable achievements, considered a miracle by many, came in Calcutta in 1947 as India was just beginning her independence. Hindus and Muslims, having a long history of animosity, began slaughtering one another and the city fell into massive riots. Gandhi entered Calcutta and announced that he would fast unto death unless the leaders of the opposing factions ceased hostilities and signed a peace agreement.

After several more days of bloodshed, word spread that the Mahatma (Great One) was dying. A hush seemed to fall over the city. The leaders came together and a peace accord was signed. One small, aging and fragile yogi had pierced the hearts of his countrymen and ignited their higher awareness to a level that shifted them into Ahimsa. As Gandhi illustrated, non-violence has the inherent energy of a higher moral principle and the power to overcome the mightiest of foes, especially the foe within us.

Ahimsa not only asks us to be committed to direct non-violence, but also to not abet or profit from violence in any indirect way. In today's world, this goes as far as liquidating any holdings we might have in stocks or mutual funds that profit from war, plundering the environment or exploiting Third World labor and resources. It becomes as subtle as realizing that if we eat too much food and acquire too many possessions we are harming both ourselves and the resources of Mother Earth, leaving us out of balance and in disharmony with Yoga. Even using mainstream, toxic household cleansers and detergents is a form of harming our own living spaces and the earth around us as these toxins go down our drains and find their way into nature.

Ahimsa is also why Yoga promotes vegetarianism. There is obvious violence in the killing of animals for our food. Countries with diets based upon heavy meat consumption are historically more violent than countries where vegetarianism predominates. Ayurveda, the sister science of Yoga designed to promote physical and mental wellness as a prelude to the spiritual ascent of Yoga, holds that not only is a heavy diet of meat at the root of most disease, it also causes us to become more agitated, aggressive and violent through its consumption.

Factory farms are notorious for the violence committed against the animals they raise, which are also typically pumped full of hormones, antibiotics and toxic foodstuffs. Similarly, farm-raised fish are often filled with antibiotics and the artificial environment degrades their quality as a food product. Not only are these products toxic, they carry the *karma*, or consequences of past actions, of the violence typically employed in these industries. Moreover, the consumption of meat has a remarkably deleterious impact upon our environment, as detailed in Chapter Eight.

Ahimsa is a challenging principle to live by in our culture, which is permeated by direct and subtle forms of violence. We are a warlike nation. Our history is replete with examples of our using force to impose our will around the globe for our own personal benefit. Our movies and television dramas glorify conflict and violence. It is a centerpiece of print and broadcast journalism. Violence permeates much of the lyrics in the music popular with our youth. Anger, a subset of violence, runs like a deep current in our collective mind. It manifests in phenomena such as road rage and domestic abuse.

To stand in Ahimsa requires profound courage and a willingness to endure the ridicule of those intoxicated by drama, anger and conflict. It means a commitment to live our lives using fewer of the Earth's resources, and perhaps having lower returns from our investments while paying more for what we do need to ensure it comes from mindful producers. It means tuning out the violence of mass media and not engaging in negative speech, profanity or gossip. It means being ever mindful and noticing the subtler forms of violence and harming around us and then acting accordingly.

It is human nature that anger will arise at times for all of us. When this happens, we must first seek to see it for what it is and not try to simply bottle it up or pretend that we are not having these feelings. By the act of contemplating what pushes our buttons we can begin to release and reprogram ourselves into higher states of awareness. It may take months or years to truly diminish the level of violence within us, but the benefits of such effort are profound.

Perhaps most importantly, Ahimsa also involves practicing non-harming towards our selves. When we allow "the great critic" in our minds to constantly demean us, to tell us we are unworthy or incapable, or to give us excuses for not moving forward, we are committing a form of self-violence. Yoga teaches us that we all have an incredible inner power no matter what past suffering or abuse we have experienced. Through embracing this energy we have the capacity to heal, to grow and to transform our lives in a multitude of ways. Our culture and economy have sought to disempower and disenfranchise us, making us lose faith in our abilities and leaving us dependent upon external remedies that perpetually fall short of their promises. Practicing Ahimsa means accepting and embracing ourselves just as we are in the present moment while resolving to move forward with faith, courage, confidence and conviction.

In the Bhagavad-Gita that so informed the life of Mahatma Gandhi, the mythical warrior Arjuna is standing on the battlefield of his life despairing over the imminent conflict he is facing. His charioteer, Krishna, an embodiment of the Divine, rebukes him in his moment of doubt, telling him to stand firmly in the principles of Yoga as he vanquishes his "dark side." Each of us is like Arjuna, facing the challenges of our conditioning, habits, inhibitions and lack of resolve. Krishna is the voice of our deeper self, that inner knowing in our heart of what we can and must do to manifest our fullest potential. And while the Gita is set in a military battle that seems to contradict the principles of Ahimsa, it is actually about the inner struggle we all face to overcome our demons and live in peace, harmony and grace.

Ahimsa Practice

To enhance your awareness and practice of Ahimsa, I invite you first to contemplate any and all aspects of violence, anger and harming, from the gross to the subtle, which might be in your life. As you do, journal what comes up for you and organize your list in terms of your priorities for change. Then begin by dealing with any aspects of your self-image that need healing. Practice letting go of self-doubt, judgment or condemnation and begin to cultivate self-acceptance, confidence and love on a daily basis. Resolve not to engage in gossip or speak profanities. Set aside a specific time each day for this practice, even if it is only a few minutes. Breathe peace in and breathe peace out, especially when you are most agitated.

Next, prioritize ways in which you can move more deeply into Ahimsa. There is no set order here. Some might want to begin with disassociating themselves from companies or products that profit from violence or harming, others might work on their own anger or tuning out the violence of mass media and mindless speech. The key is to cultivate a mindfulness of these things so that we began to see them more clearly, then learning to act accordingly.

The flame that burns brightly at the very core of Ahimsa is the flame of **Shanti**, or peace. Look for ways that you can contribute to peace, no matter how simple they might be. This might involve donating your time to organizations that promote peace or helping victims of violence or social disenfranchisement. It might be something simpler, with less structure, such as doing all you are able to be the most peaceful person you can be. The more we bring peace into our lives and into the world around us, no matter how small or humble our efforts, the more we unlock the mighty power of Ahimsa and help ourselves, and the world around us, to heal.

*If we firmly establish ourselves in truth,
we no longer need worry
about sustaining deceptions
or what the consequences
of being discovered might be.
We move further from ignorance
and closer to the Divine.*

CHAPTER THREE
Satya

In 1922 a miraculous invention was unveiled through which the human voice could be broadcast over great distances. It was called the radio. Its debut came shortly after World War I as the politics of aggression began spreading through Europe. The Nazis rising in Germany, Communists in the Soviet Union, and Fascists in Italy all found that this new technology was a perfect tool for the dissemination of propaganda and to control the "group mind" of their citizens. This in turn led to totalitarian domination of political and economic power.

A key to the success of this propaganda was making falsehoods seem true. Through well-crafted lies, these regimes could foment hatred and illusion, setting the stage for manipulation, exploitation and war. While radio was the method for disseminating this propaganda, it was the seminal work of Sigmund Freud in the field of psychoanalysis and human behavior that provided the techniques.

As World War II approached, the Nazis embraced Freud's theories on how the mind could be programmed and controlled by others in a deceitful and perverse way, then used these techniques to manipulate the German public into supporting mass genocide against the Jews. This was not only insidious, but ironic as well since Freud was Jewish and would never have dreamed that his life work would be used for mass genocide, especially against his own people.

Shortly thereafter, a nephew of Freud's named Edward
Bernays developed "psychology-based communication,"
creating a modern science of mass persuasion based upon
his uncle's seminal work. Bernays realized that the subconscious feelings and impulses manipulated so successfully by
the Nazis also could be used to control behavioral patterns
of personal consumption. This offered the possibility of increased business profits, and the potential for great financial
rewards for Bernays.

Now known as the Father of Public Relations, Bernays left
Austria and immigrated to the United States before the Nazis
swarmed Europe. His work in America transformed commercial advertising and the process of political persuasion.
In his book entitled "Propaganda," published in 1928,
Bernays postulated, *"If we understand the mechanism and motives
of the group mind, is it not possible to control and regiment the
masses according to our will without their knowing about it?"*

Bernays realized that the media, especially with television
entering the scene in the late 1930s, could be used to create profound subconscious desires that would serve to enrich
corporate concerns. Further, bogus or manipulated news
events could be staged to increase public appetites. From
this arose the credo that still governs marketing to this day,
"create a need and then fill it."

One of Bernays' first great "successes" was for the American Tobacco Company. At that time, most American wom-
en would not smoke because cigarettes were perceived as
phallic symbols of male power and therefore inappropriate
and vulgar for women. But women were beginning to assert
themselves in our biased culture and seek equality, especially
through demanding the right to vote.

These activists called themselves Suffragettes. At the height of their movement, they held a march down New York's Fifth Avenue in a parade for women's rights. Exploiting this event, Bernays hired a group of attractive actresses to pose as Suffragettes and join the protest. As they marched past news photographers, Bernays' impostors pulled out and lit American Tobacco Company cigarettes, proclaiming them "torches of freedom."

It worked. With media coverage and subsequent advertising, women across the country began to equate smoking with asserting their rights to equality. Their reason had been clouded over by desire and illusion planted in their consciousness... a desire to look as glamorous as the actresses posing as Suffragettes, and the illusion that smoking would make them strong and independent, belonging to a new wave of modern, assertive women. As predicted, their minds were controlled and regimented without their ever realizing it. One can only wonder how many American women have subsequently suffered and died from lung cancer as a result of Bernays' deceptions and the tobacco industry's sustained lies denying the dangers of cigarettes.

The second of the five Yamas is *Satya*, or truthfulness. The golden flame at the heart of Satya glows with love, compassion and integrity. The mind in the brain, with all of its turbidity, often clouds Satya, but the wisdom of the heart is ever pure and truthful. The instinctual knowing that we all have deep within us is the voice of our Soul. It is ever honest, incorruptible and eternal. You've heard it every time you have engaged in unconscious behavior, even if you chose not to listen. As we seek to still the mind in our head, we hear this whisper of the Soul with increasing clarity. Eventually we enter into full dialogue and live from this place of grace. The practice of Satya is a pathway to this wisdom of the heart.

Most of us have been taught since childhood to always tell the truth, but how many of us truly do? We often find it easier (or so we think) to tell little white lies to get through our days. Most of us have told larger lies in order to hide certain actions of which we were not proud or that might result in negative consequences. We might call in sick to work in order to go to a movie, leave a fact out of a document if we think it might thwart our ends, or spare our true feelings to a friend or loved one for fear of causing hurt, conflict or retaliation.

We even tell lies to ourselves about our motivations, or to excuse ourselves for inappropriate behavior. This comes in the form of rationalization and self-delusion. Extreme examples of this are the alcoholics and drug addicts who lie to themselves and others about their addictions to justify their consumption due to all of the hurt and injustice they face in their lives. This also is done on more subtle levels by millions of us to excuse over-consumption of food, chronic shopping, lack of self-discipline and other embarrassing behaviors that we are unwilling to face.

Patanjali addresses Satya in this way:

Sutra 2.36 *Satya Pratisthayam Kriya Phalasrayatvam.*

"To one established in truthfulness, actions and their results become subservient."

If we firmly establish ourselves in truth, we remove illusion, self-deceit and pretense. These are elements that veil reality, create fear and constrict the heart. When we are truthful with ourselves and with others, our actions are in alignment and the results take care of themselves. We no longer need worry about sustaining deceptions or what the consequences of being discovered might be. We move further from ignorance and closer to the Divine.

Just as we live in a culture of violence, we also live in a culture of lies, which are a subtle form of violence. The psychological manipulation that Bernays brought to America now permeates our entire culture. Advertising has become the high art of illusion, misstatement and falsehood, and is designed to create artificial desire resulting in the endless purchase of unnecessary goods and services. This chronic consumption places us at the very lowest level of consciousness, identifying ourselves as "consumers" and going through our lives on a vacuous and unrewarding quest to acquire and consume our way into relevance and satisfaction.

Mass media, which is predicated on misleading advertising and illusory images, is inescapable. Before the age of five, the average child is exposed to thousands of commercials. These slickly produced, fast-paced and seductive messages deeply influence their most precious commodity – their consciousness. By adulthood, most of us have been so saturated by these manipulative messages that the desires arising from them define our lives. We have become so thoroughly brainwashed and manipulated that we haven't a clue as to what is going on.

As Krishna admonished the warrior Arjuna thousands of years ago in the Bhagavad-Gita, *"Desire has found a place in man's senses and mind and reason, through this it blinds the soul, after having over-clouded wisdom* (III:40)." As discussed in Chapter One, Arjuna was standing on the battlefield of life, facing his own personal demons in the form of a vast army with which he would have to do battle. A central theme of this great spiritual text was the danger of desire, how far it could lead us astray, and the suffering that is sure to ensue for those of us unable or unwilling to rise above it. The wisdom that it clouds is the wisdom of truth that arises from our deeper consciousness.

Ironically, the American culture – and many others as well – is predominantly based upon creating and sustaining chronic desire to a level that was unknown so many centuries ago when the great sages warned of its dangers. Most of us have a list of desires in the back of our minds that percolates to the forefront throughout each day. We want better homes, cars, clothes, jobs, relationships and vacations. We want new and improved versions of things that we already possess. We want the latest and most fashionable accoutrements, to keep pace with our peers and neighbors, to continually be "arriving" in every way.

This chronic desire can even slip its way into our practice of Yoga, which is supposed to help us transcend desire! We can find ourselves wanting the right Yoga clothes, coveting the new mat with the OM symbol that the person next to us just bought, or thinking that a new mantra might be the key to deepening our meditation practice. Krishna would be stunned to see the level of desire that exists today and, as he advised Arjuna, would urge all of us to slay this demon so that we might live in our truth.

Much of the time we are not even aware of why we have these desires or where they come from. They are so pervasive as to seem a natural part of being alive. We feel them inside of us so we assume that they are "ours", and since they seem to have arisen from within our consciousness we feel they are valid and appropriate. Everyone we know has similar desires, and they typically dominate our casual conversations and form the focal points of our mutual bonding. But they aren't really ours. They have been created for us, through illusions and lies, and we are simply acting like puppets with an invisible puppeteer pulling the strings. However, if told our minds were under the control of mass media without us even knowing about it, that we live in an artificial bubble of social conditioning, most of us would scornfully reject this notion, firmly convinced that the desires created for us are own and willing to defend them with great vigor as central aspects of our identity.

Political campaigns, which seem almost nonstop these days, are founded on attacking opponents with twisted facts, creating illusions, massaging the truth and misrepresenting reality. We find the same prevarication in most political speeches and statements. We went to war in Iraq based upon such lies, as is so often the case in war, and continue to dodge the truth about our motives and goals there and elsewhere in the world. Truth is always the first casualty of conflict and lying is the currency of military and government propaganda. During my three decades as a broadcast journalist, I witnessed endless manipulation of news organizations by highly paid and very skillful business and political operatives who wanted to create an illusion of reality that dovetailed with their press releases and ad campaigns.

Through all of this Bernays' postulation has come true. The American masses, who largely view themselves as the most free and independent individuals on Earth, are being artfully controlled and regimented without having a clue that it is happening. This chronic desire that is being created for us, and the constant state of untruth and unhappiness that accompanies it, is at the core of our suffering. It's little wonder that millions of us take anti-depressants every day and that living in truthfulness is so challenging.

From the perspective of Ayurveda, the holistic medical system that is the sister science of Yoga, all the Prozac in the world won't help. We must take the necessary steps to remove these toxins from our consciousness, much as we would seek to remove bacteria causing a physical infection. Ayurveda holds that the vast majority of physical disease arises from mental imbalance, and it is clear that the primary source of mental imbalance in modern society is deliberately created in order to control our consciousness and behavior. As a result, we are collectively far from being sane.

To remove these mental toxins we must first remove their primary source – mass media and the attendant dishonest socialization that goes along with it. We must embrace Satya, perceive the truth and then live in it, bursting out of the bubble of these artificial conventions, transcending our desires, liberating ourselves from this brainwashing and taking back our minds so that we can set our own course in life.

Along with tuning out these falsehoods, we must seek to be as honest as possible with ourselves and with others, without being rude or overly blunt to people who might be sensitive or misunderstand. Every time we engage in behaviors or speech that are removed from the truth, there is a deep inner knowing of our transgression. While we can seek to ignore or rationalize it away, it is always there. We must strive to listen more closely to this inner voice and to unfold our truth as much as possible. This includes living our lives in the most authentic manner possible, following our inner truth in lifestyle, career and associations.

Practice

As a practice in Satya, become more mindful of all of the propaganda, falsehoods and misrepresentations around you. See them for what they are and tune them out whenever possible. If you do watch commercial television and are not ready to tune it out, notice the lack of truth and integrity in most of these messages. Look behind the words and images and see how the techniques of Edward Bernays are still being used to manipulate your consciousness. Even with this awareness, however, it is still best not to expose yourself to these false messages as they seep into the unconscious even when we are cognizant of their lack of integrity.

Also, try to notice when little lies or misstatements arise for you. Then, practice *Vichara*, the yogic form of meditation in which you actually ponder these things and look for their root causes. As you go to the core of each incident, you will begin to come to a better understanding of where it arises from and cultivate a deeper connection with your inner voice of truth. This helps bring us from thinking with our heads to the wisdom of our hearts. Realize that this process takes time, and don't punish yourself for any transgressions.

Be mindful of your speech. Do your best to be authentic as well as honest, speaking from the heart without ulterior motive. Before speaking, ask yourself: *"Is this the truth? Is it my authentic voice?"* Notice how good it feels when others are being authentic with you, and the difference you experience when they are not. Try to avoid negative conversations, gossip and idle speculation.

Contemplate what your deeper aspirations are and meditate upon them as well. Make a plan in this regard, one that will help you act more skillfully to manifest these aspirations and live more fully in your *dharma*, the truth of who you really are and what you were meant to do in this lifetime in terms of right action and livelihood.

Through this process, you will be "Living the Gita," moving away from the desire, fear and control that have left you feeling so much anxiety and agitation, and moving towards the liberating peace and contentment that is your natural state of being. Just as peace is the flame at the core of Ahimsa, it is also at the core of Satya. The sacred light of truth really does have the power to set you free.

*When we release greed, we no longer
need to steal.
When we learn to give, we no longer
need to take.
When we learn to serve,
self-centeredness dissolves
and Grace arises.*

CHAPTER FOUR
Asteya

A close friend of yours has just heard an inspirational song that lifts their spirits and makes them think of you. They received this song on a CD that a friend copied for them. They make another copy and bring it to you. You are touched by their thoughtfulness and, like them, you find this song deeply moving. You copy it to a few CDs and give them to other friends to share this beautiful experience. Your friends in turn make copies for others whom they hold dear to their hearts. And so this song spreads out to an untold number of people, most all of whom are deeply moved. It has been a wonderful sharing.

However, to the artists who composed, performed and recorded this song and whose livelihoods are connected with its sales, you and all of your friends have been doing nothing more than stealing. One little song shared with so much good intention behind it might seem like the smallest of transgressions, but it's actually part of the billion dollar copyright battle that has arisen with the advent of home computers capable of burning CDs and websites where music can be freely shared and downloaded. This is an illustration of why it is not the size of the transgression that matters, it's the principle behind it.

Just as we all are taught not to engage in overt violence or lying, we are taught *Asteya*, or non-stealing. But like the principles of Ahimsa and Satya, the Yoga of Asteya runs from the obvious to the subtle and from the personal to the universal. There are scores of ways that most of us engage in or support stealing without actually being aware of what we are doing. Yoga invites us to raise our consciousness to a level where we become increasingly aware of these subtleties and then to implement appropriate action in our lives. Patanjali addresses Asteya in this way:

Sutra 2.37 *Asteya Pratisthayam Sarva Ratnopasthana.*

"To one established in non-stealing, all wealth comes."

This is similar to the dog not biting the hand of the person established in non-violence. When we are established in the honesty of non-stealing, abundance comes our way. When we seek financial gain to the point of engaging in some form of stealing, we are likely to either not get what we were after or lose it at some point in the future. In the process, we also lose touch with our soul.

In the last chapter on Satya we discussed the illusory images and false words of mass media designed to manipulate our behavior patterns. This is also a sophisticated form of theft, designed to take our financial resources and form our patterns of consumption, opinions and political allegiances. Mass media also steals our consciousness, often with our complicity.

Just as our culture is permeated with violence and falsehood it is also awash in stealing. Americans are by far the greatest consumers on the planet. We consume most of the world's oil and other natural resources and are the largest purchasers of consumer goods. If all of the people alive today consumed at our level, it's estimated it would take the resources of six Planet Earths to meet the demand. Observing, understanding and not participating in this obsessive consumption is an essential element of practicing Asteya and moving towards the liberation of Yoga.

The resources of Mother Earth are finite and sacred. When we turn too many of them to our individual use, especially for things we truly don't need and often discard or store away after brief enjoyment of them, we are stealing these sacred resources. This is a theft both from Mother Earth and from the less fortunate, who comprise the vast majority of humankind. Most of us are also storing and keeping things that might be put to good use by those truly in need and by organizations that serve the poor.

When governments spend billions of dollars waging war but do not attend to the feeding or education of the poor, it is stealing. When land is appropriated at the expense of the general public for the use of the wealthy, privileged and politically powerful, it is stealing. When we seek to profit at anyone else's expense, it is stealing. When a nation's economy is predicated upon consuming, such as most capitalist economies, it fosters the greed, self-centeredness and over-indulgence from which stealing arises.

At the core of this aspect of Asteya is greed. Our culture is awash in greed, which is nourished by stealing. The top one percent of America's wealthy control more than one third of the nation's privately held wealth. The average CEO makes 400 times what he pays his workers. Money has become the primary focus of worship in our society, and the greed this creates has diminished our integrity. It is a greed that arises from desire, which, as we have seen, is predominantly a creation of mass media that permeates our collective consciousness. As my teacher, Dr. David Frawley puts it in his book

Yoga and Ayurveda, "true willpower is not measured by the ability to get what we want, but by our ability to transcend desire. Desire is not the result of our free choice. It is a compulsion that comes to us from the external world, a kind of hypnosis."

To move beyond such desire, greed and theft we must first begin by seeing the subtle manifestations of it in our individual lives and seek to move beyond it. Just as we find ourselves telling many little white lies for what we think is convenience's sake, it's likely that we commit little thefts without paying attention. For instance, along with burning and sharing CDs of music without paying the artist, we might take home a magazine from a physician's waiting room, or keep a nice little item that we find somewhere without trying to contact the person who lost it or turn it in. While these might seem like small and insignificant transgressions, they add up over time and erode our moral fiber.

Stealing also can be much more subtle. If we keep our car engine running at the drive-up bank teller window or while waiting for our children at school, it is a wasteful theft of precious resources. Driving when we could walk or ride a bike, using plastic bags for our groceries instead of reusing bags we already have, or leaving lights on in rooms when we depart are all forms of theft. The same holds true for letting the water run as we brush our teeth or taking long showers. All of this wasting, upon which the Green Movement is based, is a form of stealing. The act of "going green" in our lives is an act of Asteya. It is the Yoga of Mindfulness.

It is important, as well, to take into account how and where the goods we do choose to purchase are created. Many multinational companies that pour inexpensive goods into the marketplace exploit foreign labor and resources. They have cozy relationships with dictatorial regimes that keep their people in poverty in order to create desperate work forces willing to put in long hours for low wages. These governments and corporations are involved in a partnership of stealing from the poor and disenfranchised so as to enrich themselves. When we purchase their products we are aiding this practice. In effect, we are stealing by proxy, and contributing to violence as well. This can be as subtle as the violence of human exploitation or the direct violence of suppressing labor movements and assassinating popular leaders seeking social equality for the masses.

It is challenging to determine which companies are involved in these practices since much of the intricacies of global trade are deliberately obscured. But a close look at most multinational corporations will reveal the pervasiveness of the problem. Also, as a general rule, more mindful companies usually make a point of informing consumers of all of the contents of their products, how they identify and support the labor force that produces them, and what they do to ensure they are both environmentally and politically green. To practice Asteya, we must be willing to both enhance our awareness, do the necessary research and work to live more consciously in this regard.

On an emotional level, if we spend too much time seeking validation and comfort from others and making a drama of our petty concerns, we are engaging in emotional theft. We are stealing the energy and attention of family and friends when we should be trying to understand the lessons of our situation and seeking to make appropriate shifts in our lives. This doesn't mean we should not rely upon those close to us in times of crisis, but we should be mindful not to make this a chronic habit in times that fall short of true crisis. When we fall out of Asteya, we are also stealing from ourselves. Each time we knowingly commit or participate in stealing, no matter how small, benign or easy to rationalize, we are stealing our own integrity. Our integrity is a precious treasure to be guarded with loving care. As we diminish it, we diminish our self-esteem. Lower self-esteem in turn creates more imbalanced behavior, less concern about the way in which we live our lives and less compassion for the wellbeing of others. It is this individual mindset that leads to the national mindset of stealing and exploitation outlined earlier in this chapter.

From a health standpoint, the mental imbalances that arise from violence, untruthfulness and stealing inevitably create a more disturbed mind. This increases stress and ignites the emotions of anger and fear. As Ayurveda teaches us, and modern medicine is now confirming, chronic stress and negative emotions are the root causes of most physical illness. The physical and mental bodies are not separate. An imbalanced and unhealthy mind leads to an imbalanced and unhealthy body, and vice-versa. This is why traditionally Ayurveda is practiced first, as a holistic pathway towards vibrant mental and physical health, before the deeper spiritual practices of Yoga are undertaken. In this context, both the Yamas and Niyamas are as much Ayurvedic medicine as they are core components of Yoga.

Practice

As a practice, seek to grow your awareness of how stealing permeates our culture. Resolve to do your best not to purchase goods or services from companies that lack moral integrity.

Each time you decide to make a purchase, ask yourself if you really need this particular item or if your decision arises from a desire that has been created for you or as a result of old habit patterns. Just as we should not invest in stocks or mutual funds that benefit companies that are engaged in violence, we should not involve ourselves with those that steal. Usually they are one and the same. There are many socially and environmentally conscious "green funds" available today that do the investigative work for us. While your financial returns might be a bit lower, you will reap great rewards in terms of being more mindful, raising your consciousness and entering the harmony and grace of Yoga.

On a more personal level, try to become more aware of small, subtle ways that you fall out of Asteya in your life, then do your best to put an end to these habits and live in greater personal integrity. Use less gas and electricity. Be mindful of the preciousness of water. Remember that all materials arise from Mother Earth and are both precious and sacred. Be aware and sensitive to not stealing the emotional energy of others as well. Over time, these little habits of subtle stealing will be replaced by patterns of mindfulness and Asteya. From this arises a true comfort and inner peace that help sustain us on our journey into Yoga.

*We should live to the fullest
and rejoice
in every single moment.
It is when we become attached to our senses,
seeking fleeting pleasure only through them
and habitually overindulging ourselves,
that we endanger our wellbeing.*

CHAPTER FIVE
Bramacharya

Visualize a thick, tall candle with a golden flame. Now, imagine the radiance of this flame is like your inner light: shining brightly and illuminating the world around you. The flame itself is your inner power: concentrated and hot, filled with strength and vigor. The wax of the candle is your source of fuel: thick, substantial and lasting. This candle, with its flame and light, is a metaphor for the Ayurvedic concept of our Vital Essences.

Ayurveda is based on the *Doshas*, the three primary forces in the body called *Vata, Pitta* and *Kapha*. They are considered the main forces and subtle substances behind all physiological and psychological functions. We all have a primary, or dominant Dosha, although some of us are considered bi-Doshic or tri-Doshic. Factors of our lifestyle and social conditioning tend to aggravate the Doshas, which in and of themselves are considered imbalances. Ayurveda seeks to bring them back into balance through a host of techniques, including diet, herbs, lifestyle and mental attitude.

Behind the Doshas are their subtler forms, or Vital Essences, known as *Prana, Tejas* and *Ojas*. These essences exist in the subtle and causal bodies – the mental and pranic fields – and are considered the positive side of the Doshas. Prana is our life force and gives vitality to the mind. Tejas gives intelligence, courage, self-discipline and passion. Ojas provides strength, fortitude, endurance and a strong immune system.

Returning to the candle metaphor, Prana is the glow of the flame, Tejas is the flame itself, and Ojas is the wax that sustains the flame. It is primarily Ojas that Patanjali is addressing with the Yama of *Bramacharya*.

Sutra 2.38 ***Bramacharya Pratisthayam Virya Labhah.***

"For one established in continence, vigor is gained."

Virya means vital energy. Labha means profit. We profit through retaining our vital energy. Conversely, we suffer through squandering it. The spiritual journey of Yoga takes great mental and physical strength. Without it we are unlikely to reach our intended destination. Hence, it is essential to build and retain our vital essences, especially our Ojas.

The most powerful form of our Ojas is called *shukra*, which is our reproductive tissue and fluids. It is obviously the essence of life and procreation. The word shukra means both "seed" and "luminous," and is also the Sanskrit name for the planet Venus. Shukra provides strength, energy and stamina for the entire body. When our shukra is low our capacity to perform is diminished, our creativity is lessened and our mind is directly impacted. We not only become impotent in terms of creating new life, we reduce the potency of our own lives as well.

Bramacharya includes the practice of retaining our shukra. Many have taken this throughout the ages to mean that sex must be abstained from altogether. While such abstention may well be beneficial for those pursuing a completely monastic life, it is too extreme for the majority of us. Such severe practice can also become a form of fanaticism and fundamentalism, and as such serves more to constrict rather than liberate us.

Sexuality is not only natural, it one of the most potent and powerful aspects of existence. We have seen examples throughout history of how the suppression of this natural urge has led to derangement. Recent sex scandals have plagued the Catholic Church, and the problem has not escaped the Yoga community. Most of these problems have arisen as a result of spiritual leaders preaching abstinence while sexually indulging themselves behind the scenes.

We should not seek to follow any overly rigid dogma concerning sex or embrace a practice that denies an essential aspect of our being. Tantric and Hatha Yoga, for example, detail practices for having intercourse with full consummation yet retaining all sexual fluids. We should, however, be mindful of how our vital energy is expended. The most natural way is in an intimate and meaningful relationship. Even here, moderation is advised. Returning to the candle analogy, our Ojas becomes the flame of our Tejas, which in turn becomes the radiant light of our Prana. The more we cultivate and retain, the more we become radiant beings.

In a broader context, Bramacharya is a practice of moderation and abstention, especially when it comes to indulging all of our senses. Just as we have noted the many ways that violence, dishonesty and stealing pervade modern culture and contribute to our conditioning, sensual pleasures are a major focus of society and economics. From early childhood we are taught to focus on and cultivate our desires. We learn to associate gifts and acquisition of material items with affection and love. We are tantalized with sweets to the point that food often becomes more about pleasure of the senses than nourishment of the body. Mass media and computer technology offer endless seductive distractions predicated upon stimulating our senses. By adulthood most of us are deeply focused upon our external senses and ways in which we can distract ourselves through fleeting pleasures. Millions of us have the TV or radio on for hours each day, go to shopping malls and hunt for treasure when there is nothing there we truly need, and engage in lengthy conversations of little substance. There are multi-billion dollar industries based upon gambling, sex, movies, alcohol, vacations, parties and other distractions, all based upon pleasing our senses. These are the modern manifestations of the same desires that Krishna warned Arjuna to avoid in the Bhagavad-Gita.

Verse II:48 *"Do thy work in the peace of Yoga and, free from selfish desires, be not moved in success or failure. Yoga is evenness of mind, a peace that is ever the same."*

Desire has a wide range of impacts upon us depending upon how much we cater to our baser urges and compulsions. Over-shopping or too many vacations can deplete our economic security. Overeating or excessive drinking diminishes our health. Vicarious living through mass media deranges our minds. The extreme examples of this are the lives ruined by drug addiction or alcoholism, the pervasive health crisis of obesity and the financial ruin of compulsive gambling.

This is not to say that we should withdraw into a cave and chant OM for the rest of our lives without having any other experiences. We should live our lives to the fullest and rejoice in every single moment, exploring and absorbing all aspects of our existence. It's when we become attached to our senses, seeking fleeting pleasure only through them and habitually overindulging ourselves, that we endanger our wellbeing. From an Ayurvedic viewpoint, this is a primary cause of imbalance and disease.

From a spiritual standpoint, through embracing Bramacharya we retain our precious vital essences and use them for more meaningful pursuits. A lack of Bramacharya in our lives moves us in the opposite direction of Self-realization. We become completely identified with sensory input and the thought-stream in our minds. We forget who we truly are. We suffer. The Sutras refer to this as the Kleshas, or obstacles to Yoga.

Sutra 2.3 *Avidyaasmita Raga Dvesabhinivesah Klesha.*

"Ignorance, egoism, attachment, aversion and fear are the five obstacles."

Avidya is the first klesha. Vidya means wisdom in Sanskrit. Placing an "A" in front of it reverses the meaning, similar to symmetrical and asymmetrical in English. Avidya, therefore, means ignorance. It is not meant as an insult or inference that we lack basic intelligence, it means we have forgotten who we truly are.

Yoga teaches us that what we are not the body or the mind, not our names or occupations, not our gender, race or nationality. We are embodiments of the Divine and Eternal. When we forget this we become overly identified with the senses and our minds. Most of us never learn this in the first place since we have largely forgotten who we are on a collective basis. This lack of knowing sets the stage for the next four Kleshas.

The second klesha is *asmita*, or egoism. When we forget that each and every one of us arises from the same Eternal

Self, we come to believe that life is all about our individual perceptions and needs. It is our movie and we are the central character, us against everyone else, our desires and their fulfillment the paramount concern in our lives. Western culture glorifies asmita in this regard with its concentrated focus on the individual and the pursuit of our desires. Most of us are convinced that we are our ego and would be little more than robotic clones without it. We revel in our self-centered dramas and allow them to define our lives.

This egoism brings the next two Kleshas of *raga* and *dvesa*, or attraction and aversion. In raga, we are continuously seeking to satisfy our desires, ever wanting to obtain more possessions, wealth, experiences and pleasurable sensations. In dvesa, we assiduously avoid all experiences we think might create displeasure, such as struggles, hardships, loss of our possessions or damage to our career, image, social status or sense of prestige.

Finally, we experience *abhinivesa*, or fear. Forgetting that we are embodiments of the eternal, we fear death. We fear losing our possessions, our wealth, self-image or social status. We fear facing uncertainty, handling change or failing in the eyes of others. This fear makes us less likely to fully express ourselves or take chances. We become constricted, embracing irrelevant social norms so as to be anonymous and therein live in mediocrity.

The five Kleshas result in *dukkha*. Dukkha is pain and suffering. It manifests as the anxiety and discomfort that most of us feel in the background of our awareness. It often causes us to seek even more distraction and pleasures of the senses, which in turn increases our dukkha and leads to millions of us taking anti-depressants for much of our lives. This is why Bramacharya is so essential to Yoga. To come home to our hearts, to that Divine Light that dwells within us, we must remember who and what we truly are. We must see our attractions and aversions for what they are, release our fears and transcend our egos. This does not mean we will become robots with no identity. It means we reclaim our true identity, extract ourselves from the bubble of social conditioning and self-indulgence, and live our lives as free souls.

Practice

As a practice, seek to notice what your desires are. Are there ways in which you habitually indulge these desires that are not in your best interest? Can you begin the process of not responding to them and shifting towards more positive behaviors that won't deplete your vital being? Come to understand as well that most of your desires are not truly yours. They have been created for you and sustained through socialization and mass media. Begin to notice the difference between an authentic aspiration that arises from the heart and a habitual desire that comes from the brain.

Notice, too, when certain situations or environments feel as if they are depleting your Vital Essences, especially your prana. You'll likely find that harsh lights, loud noises, aggressive music and large, stressed-out crowds are depleting. Parties where people drink too much alcohol, speak without authenticity or gossip recklessly, are also depleting. You may find it draining as well to be in social situations that seem to prohibit you from being your true Self.

Notice also those environments and activities that seem to nourish you. You'll find most of these are in nature, where things are in balance and more serene. Truly meaningful and conscious company enhances our vital essences, as does regular attendance at well-guided Yoga asana classes, kirtans (chanting) and meditations. Retreats can be the most nourishing of all, and serve as reminders of the true beauty and sacredness of life.

Do your best to avoid depleting situations and increase your commitment to experiences and environments that nourish you. Find time to do nothing except to just be fully in the present moment. This is a natural way to practice Bramacharya, and will also enhance your ability to hear the whisper of your Soul.

To live from the heart,
as mindfully as possible
and in a
spirit of loving kindness,
we must face all aspects of
greediness within us and be willing to make
the necessary changes.

CHAPTER SIX
Aparigraha

If you have a place to call home, an automobile, some savings in the bank and food in your refrigerator, you are far more fortunate than the vast majority of humankind. Tens of thousands of us die each day from hunger or hunger-related disease. Most are children. Hundreds of millions of our brothers and sisters live under tyranny and face chronic epidemics and deprivation on a daily basis. Half the world, more than three billion of us, survive on less than two dollars per day. Yet it is often too easy for us to take the abundance in our lives for granted and continually covet more.

While we may not be aware of it, this materialistic desire is a manifestation of greed. The axis of America's economy, Wall Street, runs on greed. The paradigm is to maximize profits in every way possible, often at the expense of humankind and Mother Earth. In the classic movie, *Wall Street*, actor Michael Douglas won an Oscar for Best Actor portraying arbitrageur Gordon Gekko, who coined the phrase, "Greed is Good." This statement became so popular that it actually became a successful recruitment tool for the investment banking industry, as if it were fashionable and hip to be completely self-possessed and consumed with greed.

Over the past several decades we have seen real-life Gordon Gekkos amass great fortunes and revel in the fame and power of their wealth only to be undone in the end by their own corruption and deceit. Society embraces the accrual of

wealth as a primary gauge of success, social status and perceived intelligence. We have become so attached to money
and possessions that for many it defines our very being. This
is why economic downfall often brings suicide along with it,
such as Wall Street bankers jumping out of their office win-
dows at the advent of the Great Depression.
Contrast this with someone like Mother Teresa. This
small, humble woman came to be the very symbol of service
and devotion to humankind. For more than forty years she
ministered to the poor, sick, orphaned and dying in Calcutta, India, with rarely a thought for herself. In 1979 she was
awarded the Nobel Peace Prize for her efforts and became
internationally famed as a humanitarian for the poor and the
helpless. Ultimately, she established more than five hundred
missions in over one hundred countries. Her name today
evokes an archetype of compassion, generosity and love.
To live from the heart, as mindfully as possible and in a
spirit of loving kindness, we must face all aspects of greediness within us and be willing to make the necessary changes.
This is the practice of *Aparigraha*.

Sutra 2.39 *Aparigraha Sthairye Janmakathamta Sambodhah.*

*"When non-greed is confirmed, a thorough illumination of the
how and why of one's origin arises."*

Patanjali is telling us in this sutra that when we let go of
greed we come to understand the true meaning of our birth
and our existence. We realize that life is not all about what's
in it for us. From this awareness compassion arises, along
with understanding, acceptance and generosity. When we
release greed we are more likely to give rather than to take, to

shift away from focusing on our desires and petty concerns, and to seek to serve others less fortunate than ourselves. Practicing Aparigraha helps us to release the self-centeredness of the ego, and brings us closer to understanding the oneness of humankind.

While a foreign correspondent, I witnessed the suffering of humanity in various places around the world. I have vivid memories of children starving in Africa, refugees in Afghanistan, destitute villages in North Korea, teenagers enslaved by the drug trade in South America and young women trapped in the sex trade in Thailand. One image I will never forget comes from the Philippines.

Outside the main city of Manila there is a huge dumpsite. It covers acres of hills and canyons in a wasteland where the tropical trees and plants have been razed. A thick, hot and humid air holds the rising stench like a filthy blanket. The decaying garbage creates hot spots with smoke plumes. Wild pigs and dogs compete with large vultures for scraps of putrid food. And so do people... several hundred people who have lived in the city dump for generations, swarming each arriving truck to scratch through its garbage for anything they might eat or sell.

I went to this dump to do a story on a group of international nurses and doctors who had established a small facility on the edge of the dump to help these people cope with constant illness and disease. It looked like Dante's inferno to me. Trucks would arrive and literally dump their steaming garbage atop these people, who would then sift through it furiously while staving off the wild animals.

The garbage at the dump was so deep and thick that many had simply bored down into it and made their homes in makeshift tunnels and caves. When the first truck arrived the morning I was there, two small children, a girl of no more than four and a boy of about three, crawled out of one such hole with tattered plastic bags clutched in their tiny fists and began scurrying between the legs of the adults to grab anything they could. I chose to focus my story on them.

These children had no parents. They made eye contact with no one. Their entire world was their small cave in the garbage and the arrival of each truck. They were holding onto the very edge of survival and the aid workers on site noted that it was likely they would succumb to disease and exposure within a year or two at best. When they died, the dogs and vultures that seemed to be keeping a special eye on them would consume their corpses. They would not be the first or the last to suffer this tragic fate.

As we were departing after completing our filming, I watched the little girl stumble along a dead-end path through the steaming garbage, her tattered plastic bag filled with a few rotten items. She was wearing a ragged blouse that she had found, covered with once vibrant, traditional Filipino weaving. Historically, these colorful clothes denoted the village and tribe one belonged to and symbolized a sense of pride, identity and belonging. For her, the blouse had no meaning other than providing a little protection from the elements. As she disappeared into a smoky haze, with no true village, no culture or tribe, my heart broke. She seemed to symbolize the suffering of every child in the world and the hopelessness so many face as a way of life.

Aparigraha involves not just transcending our individual greed, but also opening our eyes and our hearts to the suffering of humanity. The more we take of the world's resources for ourselves, the less others have. The average American family consumes an amazingly disproportionate percentage of the world's resources. It's estimated that if the more than six billion people in the world consumed at this same level, it would take six Planet Earths to meet the demand. This is a fundamental reason for conflict and war, which also arise from greed.

Just as with the other Yamas, falling out of balance with Aparigraha can manifest in both obvious and extremely understated ways. Hoarding is a subtle form of greed. Consider for a moment the contents of your closets, garage and other storage areas. If you are like most of us, you will agree that you have far too much stuff. While this is not an overtly immoral or criminal act, it arises from the greed that has been imposed upon us by consumer consciousness and mass marketing. It is a form of external obesity, and just as obesity in the body causes a host of health problems, this external heaviness impacts our mental balance and wellbeing.

Most consumer-oriented nations are like our storage spaces at home, stuffed with possessions of questionable value and little relevance to our lives. A quick visit to any shopping mall quickly illustrates this point. Providing storage space for this excess has become a multi-billion dollar business in several nations. Just as Americans are the most overfed, overweight and obese people in the world, we over-consume and hoard possessions and our minds are stuffed with commercial messages, dramas and useless thoughts. Aparigraha is a form of fasting from all of this, a purgation of the toxicity of over-consumption and greed.

Together, greed and stealing are co-conspirators that sabotage the Soul. Asteya and Aparigraha are the spiritual medicines that heal us from these pandemic maladies. Looking more deeply, we can see how the Yamas overlap and intertwine, bringing us to greater awareness and conscious living. For instance, overeating, mentioned under Asteya in Chapter Four as a form of stealing, is also a sign of greed. Overindulging our senses, noted under Bramacharya in Chapter Five, denotes both stealing and greed. We also can see that there is harm in this stealing, overindulgence and greed, so we must practice Ahimsa, or non-violence, as well. Satya, or truthfulness, includes the practice of clearly seeing our actions and lifestyles for what they are. As we become aware of this overlap, we begin to experience the synergy of healing that arises from embracing all of the Yamas and working with them as a group.

Practice

A deeper practice of Aparigraha is to move from taking to giving. Take a close look at all those things you have stored in your home, perhaps tackling one room at a time, and give away everything you can. Relieving ourselves of the heaviness of our possessions is as healing for the subtle body as mindful dieting is for obesity. As you unburden yourself of extraneous possessions, you might notice a little voice in the back of your mind suddenly giving you convincing reasons for keeping items you haven't used in months or years. This voice comes from being programmed as consumers since childhood. It is the voice of selfishness. Try not to listen to it and stay committed to the process of giving.

Don't give certain items to friends or sell them for a small profit, as this often leads to clinging, lessens our resolve and slows down the process of releasing. Find a nearby charity and give them everything with your blessings.

Spend time each day cultivating gratitude for what you do have rather than wishing for new things. Beyond being thankful for the material abundance you enjoy, be deeply grateful for the far more important things in life that are easily taken for granted. All of Mother Nature is a sacred blessing. Water is a gift from the Divine. The sun is our center of life. The stars at night are the most magnificent show of all. Every breath we take is the greatest of all gifts and the very blessing of life itself.

We can deepen our practice through *Seva*, or selfless service to others. Donating our time to help others reminds us of the abundance we have and the lack that so many face in life. We become less self-centered and more conscious and compassionate through Seva as we learn that the greatest of gifts is in the giving, not the taking. This is the path of *Karma Yoga*, which was walked by Mother Teresa. You needn't be such a saint as she to walk by her side in your own authentic and humble way. Through this Aparigraha you will be joining countless yogis who, throughout the ages, have come to know the truth of the oneness of humankind.

*We have been conditioned
to want someone else to make the effort for us
or provide an effort-free solution.
To purify ourselves
we must rise above this conditioning,
reclaim our power
and conquer the negative habits
that are hindering us.*

CHAPTER SEVEN
Saucha

In exploring the Yamas of Ahimsa, Satya, Asteya, Bramicharya and Aparigraha, we have seen how these moral
precepts are like interwoven threads in a tapestry of mindfulness and right action. As we contemplate and practice them
we become increasingly aware of how violence, dishonesty,
stealing, self-indulgence and greed surround us, one feeding
off the other. This awakening helps us see more clearly the
social conditioning in which most of us are captive and the
multitude of ways in which it engulfs us. It also helps us see
ourselves with greater clarity and provides insight into our
own habituated patterns of thought and emotional responses
to our life experiences.

As we embrace the spiritual practice of the Yamas, we
gain a sense of clarity, vision and deeper connection with our
inner wisdom. In the process, it's important not to get full of
ourselves as a result of any personal growth we are able to
achieve, become self-righteous and superior, or judge others
for their transgressions. It is easy to fall into this trap because
the ego loves affirmation and often seeks self-aggrandize-
ment through noting the shortcomings of others. It is also a
mistake to point others out or seek to preach to them, even if
we believe we have their best interests in mind. This is never
helpful and often causes resistance and animosity. Instead,
we should stay compassionate and humble, and ever realize
that our own journey remains a work in progress.

We must also be patient and not demand instant enlightenment or go into despair when we regress. Truly embodying
the Yamas takes great time and effort, and the benefits often
come slowly. This patience is the art of *Abhyasa* and *Vairagya*,
or sustained practice with non-attachment as to the outcome.
Patanjali teaches us that this is essential to removing both
illusions and desires.

The second limb of Ashtanga is called the Niyamas. While
the Yamas are moral precepts, the *Niyamas* are personal observances. These practices guide us into living a more balanced
and harmonious lifestyle and help shape our *Sadhana*, or daily
practice. Through these observances we align ourselves more
closely with the laws of nature and bring our consciousness
closer to the Divine. In the process, we extract ourselves more
fully from the bubble of our conditioning and therein further
our journey towards liberation.

The first of the five Niyamas is Saucha, or purity.

Sutra 2.40 *Sacuat Svanga Jugupsa Parair Asamsargah.*

"From purity follows a withdrawal from enchantment over
one's own body as well as a cessation of desire for physical
contact with others."

In our teaching school, Deep Yoga, we remind students
that the body is the Temple of the Divine, a sacred vessel of
our Spirit that should be treated with awe and reverence. Why
then should we feel disenchanted about our body? I believe
what Patanjali intends is the creation of an awareness that
helps us to eventually transcend the body and move towards
seeing who we truly are. This involves moving from *Prakriti*
to *Purusha.*

Prakriti is the basic matter of which the universe consists. It is all things manifest and un-manifest, including nature and the five elements of earth, water, fire, air and space. All things in nature are ever changing. They rise and fall, just as we do in the cycle of life and death. All possessions, relationships, experiences and circumstances are in the realm of Prakriti, and therefore only temporary and ever subject to change.

Purusha is Pure Consciousness itself. It is the eternal, unchanging Cosmic Self from which our individual Spirit arises. One of the first teachings that Krishna offers Arjuna in the Bhagavad-Gita is that while the body changes from birth through childhood, adulthood, old age and death, that which animates the body does not.

Verse II:17 *"Interwoven in creation, the Spirit is beyond destruction. No one can bring to an end the Spirit which is everlasting."*

From the perspective of Yogic and Vedantic cosmology this is why it is held that we never truly die. Our body surely expires, and along with it goes the mind, the ego and the senses, but the pure light of Consciousness that animates our body persists through all eternity. It is when we become confused and identify ourselves with Prakriti rather than Purusha that we suffer Avidya, as mentioned in Chapter Five as the first of the five Kleshas, or obstacles to liberation and enlightenment. In the ignorance of Avidya we forget that we are embodiments of the Divine and become fully identified with the body, mind and ego.

This identification is a sort of enchantment with our lowest level of existence. So the Niyamas ask us to move past this physical absorption with ourselves and with others. As with the Yama of Bramacharya (abstention) in Chapter Five, we needn't literally cease all physical contact with others unless we are bent upon becoming full renunciants. It is important, however, to note if we are over-absorbed with our physical bodies and view others mostly through their physical appearances. Purification also involves actually detoxifying our bodies so as to truly honor them as Temples of the Spirit. When we purify the body we come to see the gross elements of which it is constituted, including bile, phlegm, fecal matter and undigested food, along with various other fluids, fat, tendons and sinew. This awareness helps us disassociate from any infatuation with the body and move towards a fuller understanding of who we truly are.

Physical purification is also central to the practice of Ayurveda. Techniques include strict diet and fasting along with the **Shat Karmas**, or Six Purifications of **Dhauti, Basti, Neti, Trataka, Nauli** and **Kapalabhati**. In practicing Dhauti, a long knotted cloth is swallowed and then drawn back out of the stomach. Basti is a form of herbal enema. Neti is pulling a waxed string down through each nostril and out the mouth. Trataka is prolonged gazing at a fixed point, often a candle flame. Nauli is muscular churning of the abdominal muscles. Kapalabhati is rapid bellows breathing. In the **Hatha Yoga Pradipika** additional purification techniques include ritualized vomiting to purge toxins and even the drinking of one's own urine. While most of these are radical measures, which should only be practiced under professional guidance for extreme conditions, one can quickly see how disgust for certain elements of the body might arise!

While living with terminal cancer and a failed back surgery I was given a host of pharmaceutical medications, including morphine, Prozac, Vicodin and Valium. I ate a predominantly "Western Diet" of beef, poultry and pork, with some vegetables and heavy sauces from my favorite ethnic cuisines. As a result, my body and mind were filled with toxins from the heavy drugs and impure foods. My weight soared from its normal 180-pounds to 220-plus.

When I abandoned Western medicine and embraced Yoga and Ayurveda, I experimented with many of the purifications mentioned in the Pradipika, although I could never bring myself to swallow a length of cloth or drink my own urine. As a result of these practices, along with prolonged fasting, Yoga poses, breath work, meditation and other healing modalities, I lost 80 pounds. I called this my "organic chemotherapy" and it was central to saving my life.

Only later did I come to learn that I was practicing Saucha and that I had intuitively embraced *Langhana* and *Brimhana*, or Ayurvedic reduction and tonification. Langhana was the process of reducing my bodyweight, eliminating toxins and eventually ridding myself of the cancer. Then, through Brimhana, I built back a more purified and strengthened body mass, eventually gaining 20 pounds and stabilizing at 160. This purification process, including milder variations for less acute circumstances than mine, promotes self-healing for a variety of conditions from cancer to high blood pressure, diabetes, chronic pain, obesity and more.

As we purify the body, we become stronger, suppler and more youthful, as well as healthier and happier. This process promotes greater self-esteem and confidence. It teaches us that we have the power to change our habits and transform our lives. But we must avoid the trap of becoming fixated with the body and remember that a central aspect of Saucha is to disassociate as well, again moving from Prakriti to Purusha. Patanjali addresses this in the very next sutra.

Sutra 2.41 *Sattvasuddi Saumanasyaikagryen Driyajayatma Darshana Yogyatvani Ca.*

"Moreover, one gains purity of Sattva, cheerfulness of mind, mastery over the senses and fitness for Self-realization."

Sattva, which is contained in the first word of this sutra, is one of the three components of Prakriti, along with **Rajas** and **Tamas**. These qualities, known as the Gunas, permeate all of nature, including human beings. Tamas is darkness and inertia. Rajas is action and energy. Sattva is the quality of light and love – the higher force that allows us to evolve our consciousness. Ayurveda seeks to move clients from Tamas to Rajas and then to Sattva. This is purification of all aspects of our lives, the very essence of Saucha.

While we tend to see the body and mind as separate, Ayurveda holds that they are one and the same, existing in gross and subtle form. Just as purification of the body is essential, so is purification of the mind. Remember that one of the very first sutras, mentioned in the beginning of Chapter One, is that stilling the mind leads to awareness of the Divine. Mental purification helps bring us to this stillness.

Just as overeating and impure foods pollute the body, over-ingestion of negative impressions pollute the mind. Mental purification includes recognizing these toxic impressions and fasting from them. This is why one of the main therapies we use in Deep Yoga Healing involves tuning out mass media and avoiding artificial and hectic environments. We will explore this more thoroughly in Chapter Sixteen on the Fifth

Limb of *Pratyahara*, or withdrawal of the senses.

Western medicine is predominantly allopathic and palliative. This is scientific, research-based medicine that tends to view the individual as a conglomerate of interchangeable parts and seeks to mask symptoms with medications or address them through invasive surgeries, rather than go to the root causes of our imbalances and diseases and implement appropriate remedies. My cancer was considered untreatable and the back surgery for my broken spine failed. For the physical pain I was given heavy drugs. For the emotional pain of losing my career and health in the prime of my life I was given anti-depressants. As a result, I was far worse off physically and mentally, but also far less aware of it as a result of all the drugs.

The multi-billion dollar pharmaceutical industry that has come to dominate Western medicine promises us relief without our having to make any effort. Almost every other commercial on television suggests that we can overcome impotence, anxiety, insomnia or indigestion by simply taking a pill. We see actors gorge themselves on pepperoni pizza and beer, become painfully bloated, then find instant relief by medicating themselves with little purple pills. While there are breakthrough medications that have helped save lives and combat epidemics such as malaria and polio, most modern medications merely mask symptoms and, through altering our inner chemistry, create a host of dangerous side effects. In fact, Ayurveda considers most modern pharmaceutical medications to be poison.

Yoga teaches us that we cannot have our cake and eat it too. We must go to the root causes of our mental and physical suffering and do the work it takes to purify ourselves. This is done through what I call the Cosmic Law of Opposites. Practicing the opposite of any deleterious behavior is likely to be essential to curing the malady created by that behavior. If someone is spending too much time as a couch potato and is overweight and unhealthy as a result, taking a pill won't heal them. They must turn off the TV, get up and exercise, and take responsibility for their self-healing. A depressed person must stop brooding and cultivate positive thoughts. All true healing takes effort, willpower, embracing change and fully participating in the process.

This Cosmic Law of Opposites informs the Ayurvedic principles of treating the Doshas. As discussed in Chapter Five, the Doshas are the primary constituents of the body: Vata, Pitta and Kapha. Each is considered an imbalance, and bringing them back into balance is often done through opposites.

A person with imbalanced Vata, which is the air element, is likely to have high anxiety, fear and a racing mind. Vata maladies include dry skin, indigestion and panic attacks. To balance through opposites, diet would focus on grounding foods, exercise would be stabilizing and empowering, and immersion in nature would be in peaceful settings with warmth and sunlight.

A person with imbalanced Pitta, which is the fire element, is likely to be aggressive, egotistical and controlling. Pitta diseases often involve various forms of inflammation, which is an inner fire. To balance through opposites, diets focus on mild and cooling foods, exercise is more relaxed and non-competitive, while immersion in nature focuses on water, shade and temperate climates.

A person with imbalanced Kapha, which is the water and earth elements, is likely to be lazy, unmotivated and insecure. Kapha maladies include obesity, diabetes and heart disease.

To balance through opposites, diet would be spicier and lighter, exercise would be vigorous and challenging, and immersion in nature would be strenuous hiking in mountains or deserts. All these remedies are forms of Saucha, purifying that which is impure through the Cosmic Law of Opposites. But while the cosmic law is logical and simple, its implementation is often a great challenge. We are all creatures of habit. Habits can be wonderful tools. They help us remember to brush our teeth, bathe, prepare our meals and get ourselves to work without much thinking involved. But they also can be extremely limiting and hard to break. This is why it's often so difficult to accept change such as a new job, relocation into a new neighborhood or the loss of a relationship.

Our negative habits are as deeply ingrained as our positive ones. Shifting them takes diligence, devotion and hard work. With all of our modern conveniences and the constant suggestions through mass media that we can have it all without effort or exertion, we have been conditioned to want someone else to make the effort for us or provide an effort-free solution. To purify ourselves we must rise above this conditioning, reclaim our power and conquer the negative habits that are hindering us.

Practice

To practice Saucha, always see your body as a Temple of the Divine. Realize that all food that you ingest becomes part of you. The substance of the food nourishes and becomes the body, the Prana of the food nourishes and becomes the mind. We would never vandalize or desecrate a church, mosque, synagogue or temple. These are merely architectural edifices symbolizing embodiment of Spirit. You are the real thing. Junk food and junk thoughts are a form of vandalizing this most sacred of temples.

Once a commitment to a pure diet is made, it is helpful to bless our food and cultivate gratitude towards those who have helped provide it. Periodic fasting helps eliminate toxins that often have been stored in the body for years. This should be done under the advice and guidance of an Ayurvedic practitioner. We must also fast from toxic impressions, tuning out mass media and any other situations that serve to pollute our consciousness. Some might be unavoidable, such as chronic negativity in the workplace. We can do our best not to participate in this and avoid it whenever possible by always speaking from the heart without profanities or gossip.

A daily program of Yoga poses, breath work and meditation further purifies body, mind and soul. This should be done with Ayurvedic guidance as well so that our Sadhana serves to balance our Dosha rather than aggravate it. The greatest of purifications comes from Mother Nature herself. There is profound healing medicine in immersing ourselves back into nature whenever possible, especially using the Dosha guidelines mentioned earlier. To determine your Dosha and where you might be imbalanced, Ayurvedic guidance again is advised.

Practicing Saucha is a pathway to the Divine. It harmonizes us with nature and with Spirit. Purity is always in nature, always in the Divine and always in our hearts. Through Saucha we bring the pure light of our hearts into greater fullness. Its radiance illuminates our consciousness with peace, contentment and the inner dignity that is our true essence.

*Instead of nourishing ourselves
with food from
Mother Nature
we are poisoning ourselves
with scientifically engineered, artificial foods
designed by corporate
concerns for maximum profits,
with complete disregard for the
health or wellbeing
of those who consume them.*

CHAPTER EIGHT
Purifying the Body

To delve more deeply into the purification of the physical body, this chapter focuses directly on diet. From the Yogic and Ayurvedic points of view, the choices we make about what we eat, and the relationship we cultivate with nature through our diet, are essential components of personal transformation and spiritual practice. Further, our very lives depend upon the intelligence of these choices.

Mother Nature has blessed us with an amazing array of food to nurture and sustain us, yet increasingly in our modern world it is our diet that is making us ill and actually killing us. This "Western Diet," which has been exported worldwide, is primarily based on meat, dairy, packaged, processed and junk food. Along with poisoning us, this diet also directly contributes to global warming, the pollution of our waterways, the destruction of the rainforest and the global crisis of hunger and starvation. This might seem like an extreme indictment, but the preponderance of scientific research supports these conclusions despite the aggressive opposition of the corporate food industry.

The three greatest killers in the First World - heart disease, cancer and stroke - are directly linked to the Western Diet. These "Big Three" claim some 1.5 million lives per year in America alone. This is almost 4,000 people every day of the year. The Western Diet is also a major contributor to a host of other serious illnesses from diabetes to hypertension, osteoporosis to autoimmune diseases and even mental disorders.

In fact, in the United States and most Western countries, diet-related chronic diseases represent *the single largest cause of morbidity and mortality.* This makes the "Western Diet" the greatest catastrophe we face, far beyond natural disasters, epidemic diseases or terrorism combined! Instead of nourishing ourselves with food from Mother Nature we literally are poisoning ourselves with scientifically engineered, artificial and altered foods designed by corporate concerns for maximum profits, but complete disregard for the health or wellbeing of those who consume them.

Millions of people in the First World identify deeply with their automobiles. They seek to see their own perceived self-image manifested in their vehicle, such as sporty, sophisticated, powerful, elegant or sleek. They take a great deal of time and go to great expense to keep their cars clean, polished and at their very best. Even if you are not this attached, imagine someone offering you a type of fuel for your personal automobile that reduces its performance, damages its various parts, shortens the life of its engine and costs more than regular fuel. Would you buy this product and use it? Or would you seek to stop this person from trying to foist this toxic fuel upon you or others? Now consider that most of us ingest foodstuffs on a daily basis that are as bad or worse than this hypothetical. In effect, many of us have more concern for our vehicles than for our bodies!

True food comes from nature and has no additives, requires no content labels and needs no alteration or fortification. The "Western Diet" fails to meet this definition, and it is difficult to even consider most of the contents of this diet to be food. More accurately, it is scientifically engineered foodstuff, or artificial food. Even our meat and dairy products, with the exception of a small percentage of free-range and organic producers, can no longer truly be considered food. Cattle, poultry and swine are fed unnatural diets of subsidized, genetically engineered grains (predominantly corn, soy and wheat), pickled with antibiotics since their diet and constricted, unnatural living conditions make them sick, and filled with growth hormones for maximizing their size quickly to increase corporate profits.

The packaged and processed foods that comprise most of the rest of this diet are further removed from any true definition of food. They are based primarily upon the grains used in the meat industry, with fructose, corn syrup, refined sugars, saturated oils, artificial flavorings, artificial colorings, preservatives and a host of additives that most of us cannot even pronounce much less define. In short, this multi-billion dollar foodstuff industry produces junk in pretty packages with clever advertising campaigns to convince us of its worth. We eat it and slowly get sick and die, most of us never realizing that the Western Diet is the culprit.

Of course we still have real food, which includes plants, fruits, grains, legumes, nuts and seeds. But in most supermarkets across the country you will find the real food in a small section on one end of the store, most of it inorganic, grown on contaminated soil and sprayed with pesticides and herbicides. The vast majority of the average market will be dominated by aisle upon aisle of foodstuff in boxes, cans, jars and plastic containers. Despite this artificial abundance, the food industry brings more than 17,000 new foodstuff products to market each year, with their attendant ad campaigns designed to convince us of their tastiness and nutritional value. It even pumps this junk full of allegedly nutritional additives such as vitamins, calcium and minerals to convince us it is healthy. It is not. It is deadly junk.

As a result of this artificial diet, America also has become the fattest nation on earth. Two thirds of us are overweight or obese. We suffer from a host of illnesses related to what we eat only to be prescribed an endless stream of medications meant to mask the symptoms we experience from our deranged diets. The multi-billion dollar pharmaceutical industry enjoys a symbiotic relationship with the foodstuff industry – some 70% of the antibiotics produced are for livestock – and, together with our medical system, controls much of our economy, political process and national consciousness. We eat a toxic diet which makes us sick, and see the doctor to get prescriptions for our pills. These industries literally make billions making and keeping us sick. It is in their economic interest to do so, and they have consistently waged forceful campaigns against all attempts to shift this paradigm.

We have junk food outlets at many of our schools and hospitals, with food industry "nutritionists" advising our educators and even our doctors. We then spend billions of dollars each year seeking cures for heart disease, cancer, stroke, diabetes and obesity, wondering how and why these diseases became so prevalent in the first place. The tragic irony is that we already have the cure. It is Saucha, or purity, in the form of our diet.

Returning to the harmony of eating what Mother Nature provides to us is the primary path back to balance and health. While this is logical and obvious, mainstream scientists around the globe also have proved it in study after study. Societies that eat natural, plant-based, predominantly vegetarian diets have up to 90-percent fewer of the diseases that arise from the Western Diet. When individuals from these cultures shift to a Western Diet, they eventually experience the same ailments and diseases as everyone else consuming this artificial diet.

Practicing Saucha and returning to a natural diet would save millions of lives each year in America alone. It would greatly reduce our obesity epidemic, lower medical costs and help bring health and vibrancy to our nation. Unfortunately, it would also be considered subversive and revolutionary since it would end the food, medical and pharmaceutical industries' stranglehold on our political, economic and social systems. It would require bold leaders willing to implement a national campaign to reeducate the public while resisting great pressure from corporate lobbyists. Yet it is essential that we seek to liberate ourselves from this tyranny and reclaim control over the most important aspect of our basic existence: what we eat.

Most of us have become so addicted to the taste and convenience of the Western Diet that liberating ourselves from it, even on an individual basis, seems daunting. As with any true healing and personal transformation, it does require effort (which will be more fully explored in the Niyama of *Tapas*, or self-discipline), but what is a bit of sustained effort when compared to the health, vibrancy and harmony that we can enjoy from such a shift? Do we really want to continue slowly poisoning ourselves and damaging our physical, mental and spiritual health, or do we want to take control of this most essential and fundamental aspect of our lives? The answer should be readily apparent to each and every one of us.

One of the first concerns many have about a natural, plant-based diet is getting enough protein. This "problem" is largely a myth created by the foodstuff industry nutritionists. There is more than enough protein in plants to sustain us. For instance: spinach is 49% protein, cauliflower 40%, lettuce 34% and lentils 29%. And while the meat industry claims that 40% of our diet should be protein, responsible health organizations place the figure between 2-6%. A balanced, natural diet should be based upon plant, fruits, grains, nuts, seeds and legumes. Whenever possible, these should be organic and locally grown. The further our food is shipped, and the longer it is stored, the more its Prana, or inherent life force, is diminished (this essential Prana is non-existent in processed foodstuffs). Here are a few more tips:

• Eat organic as much as possible.
• Buy locally grown food as much as possible. .
• Eat real food, not things from boxes and packages.
• If and when you do purchase packaged items, don't buy things with more than five ingredients or ingredients you cannot pronounce.
• Don't buy products with artificial colorings, preservatives or sweeteners from corn syrup or fructose.
• Focus on plants, grains, nuts and seeds, not pastas, breads, cakes and other such "fillers."

The impact of the Western Diet on global warming, world hunger, our polluted waterways and the plight of the rainforest is equally as alarming as its impact upon our health.

Every minute some 25-50 acres of rainforest is cut or burned to the ground. Most of it is for grazing cattle. For every hamburger, 55 square feet of rainforest is destroyed. The leading cause of deforestation and species extinction worldwide is livestock grazing.

Twenty-five percent of the methane produced in the world comes from livestock. Methane and carbon dioxide are the leading causes of global warming. Along with methane, 150 pounds of carbon dioxide is released into the atmosphere for every hamburger that is made. This is 25 times more carbon dioxide than you would release into the atmosphere by driving your car all day long.

Thirty percent of the pollution in our waterways comes from livestock farming. The production of one pound of beef requires 2,500 gallons of water. The production of one pound of wheat or potatoes requires only 815 gallons. If we all ate a predominantly vegetarian diet we would reverse the pollution and loss of this precious resource.

Fifteen million children die each year from starvation. This is 40,000 children every day. Every day, the world produces enough grain to provide every person on Earth with more than two loaves of bread. 40% of that grain, however, is fed to livestock. 1.4 billion people could be fed by the grain given to U.S. livestock alone. If we reduced our meat consumption by just 10%, we could feed every starving child on Earth.

Yoga and Ayurveda hold that a vegetarian diet is not only essential for our physical health, it is important for our spiritual health as well. The killing of animals is an act of violence that violates the Yama of Ahimsa, non-harming, that is the central moral precept of Yoga. Our physical relationship with nature is most fully expressed through our diet, since what we eat is what we become. Eating is a spiritual act, a merging with the very nature from which we arise.

While the practice of Yoga poses, or Asanas, is an essential component of Sadhana, or daily practice, it is not Yoga. Yoga is merging with the Divine, a coming home to the truth of who we are as embodiments of Divine Consciousness. It requires harmonizing ourselves with the Divine as expressed in the rhythms and laws of nature. It is somewhat foolish and illogical to devote ourselves to a daily regimen of Yoga poses, which – among other things – help to detoxify the body, when we are eating toxic foods day in and day out. Along with seeking to practice and live the Yamas and Niyamas, we must truly treat our bodies as Temples of the Divine Spirit that animates us.

Practice

As a practice, review your diet and note what you eat that is unnatural and would be considered less than true food. Make a plan to begin eating more healthily, choosing dietary changes that you feel you are most likely to be able to implement. Go slowly and don't try to do everything at once. Consider having a consultation with an Ayurvedic Counselor to help you formulate your plan.

As you move towards a natural, plant-based diet, here are some tips to help guide you in your choices:

• Eliminate as much meat as possible from your diet, starting with red meats.

• Focus on eating a variety of different colored, seasonal vegetables, natural grains, fresh fruits, nuts and seeds.

• Have fun with these dishes, experimenting with different spices such as cumin, coriander, turmeric and ginger.

• Remember that every meal constitutes a sacred merging between you and Mother Nature. Give thanks for this process, bless your food and feel gratitude.

• See taking charge of your diet as a centerpiece of your spiritual practice and personal transformation.

When our minds are fractured,
skittering between the
past and future,
hypothesizing, judging,
creating scenarios,
replaying loops of media images
and generally chattering away
like hyperactive monkeys,
we cannot know our True Self.

CHAPTER NINE
Purifying the Mind

Most of us have heard the poignant cliché, "you are what you eat." On the gross level, this is perfectly true. We ingest food and it becomes us. If we eat junk food and eschew exercise, the body suffers. The purer the food the purer our bodies, and the less likely we are to experience physical ailments and disease.

Another profound truth is that "you are what you think." Thought is a form of food for the mind. If we ingest a diet of "junk impressions" from mass media and fail to control our thoughts, the mind suffers. The purer our thoughts, and the purer the information we allow into our consciousness, the purer our minds. The cosmic laws governing the physical and subtle aspects of existence are one and the same.

With a pure mind we can deal with stress more readily and are able to face the challenges of our lives with greater clarity, acceptance and ease. We are less likely to suffer from the mental derangements of anger, fear and anxiety. We are able to see reality more clearly and are less affected by our preconceptions and illusions. A polluted mind, on the other hand, brings imbalance and is an obstacle to self-healing and spiritual growth.

One of the fastest growing media phenomena of the past several decades has been talk radio and TV. It is predominantly controlled by the right wing of the political spectrum, but has its left-leaning programs as well. This talk has a deep impact on our society in many ways. The hosts of these shows are intelligent and articulate. They are also arrogant, judgmental, angry and negative. They foment division, prejudice and conflict. Their opinions and projections are a highly toxic junk food for the mind. Millions of Americans listen to these programs religiously. As a result, they also become arrogant, judgmental, angry and negative. Their political opinions become social opinions and impact their relationships with family and friends. It is like a mental cancer that spreads through the collective mind of our culture, eating away at our inherent compassion and goodness.

Commercial television is equally toxic. Most popular dramas are based upon conflict, crime and sex. The explosive interactions between characters, and their dramatic responses to one another, permeate our consciousness and affect the way we perceive and interact with one another. We can tell ourselves it's only a show, but the images and words are nevertheless entering our minds and becoming part of the mental body.

The Yoga Sutras begin with the most important aphorisms of the entire text:

Sutra 1.2 *Yogas Citta Vrtti Nirodaha.*

"Yoga is stilling the fluctuations of the mind."

Sutra 1.3 *Tada Drastuh Svarupe Vasthanam.*

"Then the seer abides in his own nature."

In other words, when we still the endless fluctuations of our minds, we connect with our true and deepest Self, the Divine Being that dwells within each and every one of us. This is the absolute essence of Yoga: merging or unifying with the Divine individuated within us and with the Divine that permeates the entire Universe.

When our minds are fractured, skittering between the past and future, hypothesizing, judging, creating scenarios, replaying loops of media images and generally chattering away like hyperactive monkeys, we cannot know our True Self. This neurotic condition is the antithesis of Yoga. The vast majority of humankind is running around with this "monkey mind" day in and day out. Lost in this turbid stream of superficial consciousness, we are divorced from reality and, arguably, we are collectively insane.

Yoga and Ayurveda hold that since the mind leads to all of the choices and decisions we make in our lives, it is responsible for almost all of our mental and physical suffering and illness. We suffer most when our choices result from external influences and the whims of our senses. This suffering is called *Dukkha*, which results from the Kleshas mentioned earlier. What we do each day, based upon our minds, is truly our "spiritual practice," not what we preach, study, read or espouse. This practice is not some ritual in which we participate for an hour or two one day of the week. It is what we think and what we do each and every day of our lives.

Societies and economies with a collective "spiritual practice" predicated upon seeking wealth and consuming goods rely upon keeping our minds deranged in order to continuously sell us products and services that we don't really need. In a state of Dukkha, or anxiety, we become desperate for contentment, happiness and meaning in our lives. Mass media steps in and manipulates our minds into endless desire and coveting, promising us each time that the next acquisition or experience we purchase will bring us the peace we seek. As we all know, such promises are an illusion, a temporary distraction from our condition embodied in a material acquisition or titillation of our senses that has no lasting substance or true value.

By the time we are adults, most of us have subjected ourselves to thousands of hours of fast-paced, slickly produced and deeply seductive commercial messages. We have surrendered our consciousness to an external source in return for diversion and cheap entertainment. As a result, we have allowed our minds to be programmed at the deepest of levels. We also subject ourselves to endless media and commercialized distractions in hopes of escaping our minds. Yet most of these distractions, including computer games, shopping, watching televised dramas, mindless phone conversations and sensational movies, only serve to deepen our derangement. This is why most of us cannot focus on any one thing for more than a brief period of time, let alone begin to still our minds.

As a result of this inner turmoil most of us cannot meditate, much less get in touch with our deeper selves. We can try to meditate. With great effort, we can force ourselves to hold still for a short length of time and seek a bit more stillness, but our minds continue racing most of the time. Even many experienced meditators with decades of practice have acknowledged this to be true.

So, just as it is important to increase Saucha, or purity, in the physical body, it is also essential to seek greater mental and emotional purity. We can begin this process simply by becoming more aware of how our minds have been programmed, and how pervasive mass media is in our lives. Just as it is healthier to eat organic, fresh and wholesome foods, it is healthier to ingest impressions and experiences that are natural, authentic and peaceful.

Even if we never listened to radio or watched TV again, tuning out the media alone will not fully purify us. Unless we are hermits or aspiring sages living in caves, we interact with many other people every day. Most of them are also programmed, so the pervasive level of awareness, perspective and conversation is still dominated by the illusions created by mass media and social conditioning. Even while tuning out, we still tend to see ourselves as consumers, worrying about the economy, discussing the news of the day and generally being swept up in the wave of consciousness around us.

To deepen mental purification, it is important to create more stillness and silence in our lives, to seek to be rather than constantly do. Mother Nature also contains great healing powers. Finding more time to immerse ourselves in nature is a powerful tonic for the mind. Even in an urban or suburban environment, we can find a park to rest, or simply take a stroll and notice what plants and trees are around us, no matter how few. Deeper forays into nature, of course, are more purifying, healing and transformative.

Not only is it toxic to have a mind filled with images and impressions from external, commercial sources, it is also damaging to have consistent and ingrained negative thoughts about ourselves and others. This arises both from the mental anxiety deliberately caused by our conditioning and from our egos. As we explored through the Kleshas, when we see the world through the distorted lens of our egos we get caught up in our likes and dislikes. This causes endless judgment, attraction and aversion. It then creates fear and insecurity. Our fear leads us to seek to find fault in others so that we feel less threatened or insignificant. Then, as we are unable to control our minds and therefore find it difficult to perform at our highest level or manifest the true aspirations that we feel in our hearts, we are riddled with self-doubt and self-condemnation.

This is why we love the news. The media is always seeking to bring someone down, especially a politician, business leader or celebrity. It feeds our egos to see someone with a high life brought low. We also thrive subconsciously on news of global turmoil, cataclysmic events and natural disasters. The ego feels more secure when others are suffering. Gossip, which is often just an individualized form of what passes for news these days, is the same process. Society loves a good scandal to gossip about. Individuals often spend a great deal of time spreading the latest rumor about a friend, colleague or neighbor who has done something condemnable and can therefore be judged to the comfort of all in the group.

Cleansing this toxicity of speech is part of the purity sought through Yoga. It is better to be silent, to tune out mass media, speak no evil and work towards lessening the influence of any inner negativity. Yoga offers us a host of techniques for this part of the journey. Mantra is like a Yoga pose for the mind. It helps to still the inner dialogue and short-circuit the mental loops of our conditioning. There is also Tratak, typically practiced as gazing at a candle flame, which also helps us to focus and come more fully into the present moment. Elements of Asana, Pranayama and Pratyahara practice also help to purify the mind and release stored emotions and impressions. We will explore these elements more fully in the chapters dedicated to these limbs of Yoga.

Practice

There are several simple and obvious ways to begin purification of the mind.

- Ingest far less of what mass media is ever seeking to place into your consciousness. This is as simple as clicking off the radio and TV.
- Be more mindful of your speech. Don't use negative, harsh or profane language.
- Don't partake in gossip. Do your best to see the best in others.
- Notice when your inner judge is condemning you or others and try not to buy into this voice from the ego.
- Avoid petty distractions that you are habituated to as a way of escaping the present moment.
- Find ways to immerse yourself in Mother Nature whenever possible. Open your consciousness to her healing energies.

Simple mantras can also help purify the mind. While there are many specific mantras for a variety of purposes, these very simple ones, spoken silently to yourself, can prove to be effective and powerful when practiced with consistency.

- **OM Shanti:** *OM* is the ultimate mantra of Yoga and signifies the Divine and Eternal that underlies all that is. **Shanti** is Sanskrit for peace. Silently breath in OM and exhale Shanti, and allow yourself to feel a deeper sense of peace.
- **Om Namo:** This basically means "I bow," and when

used as an inner mantra means "I bow to the light of consciousness within me and all things." Reminding ourselves of this truth allows us to release the ego and see the bigger picture.

• **I Am**: This English mantra is very soothing, and also builds an awareness that we are Human Beings, not Human Doings.

*The key
to any lasting contentment
is learning to see
and accept reality for what it is
and then acting skillfully,
rather than reacting
when reality fails to conform
to our expectations.*

CHAPTER TEN
Santosha

All week long you've been looking forward to a Sunday pic-
nic with a few close friends. You've been stressed out, and it
seems like forever since you had a chance to relax and unwind.
You stayed up late the night before getting everything ready for
this special day. When morning comes, you jump out of bed,
throw open the curtains, and it's pouring rain outside. You
cannot believe your lousy luck and fall into a deep funk.

You are sick of your job and have been trying to find new
employment for months. Finally, you land the job interview
of a lifetime. You've prepared yourself in every way and are
ready to show your prospective employers that you are the
very best person for this position. As you pull your car out of
the garage, leaving much earlier than necessary just to ensure
you are on time, you find that you have a flat tire and there's
no spare in the trunk. You break down crying and angrily
pound your fists on the steering wheel.

You have planned to surprise your beloved with a ro-
mantic dinner. Things haven't been going so well between
the two of you and you are hoping this will rekindle your
romance and intimacy. In anticipation, you light candles,
put a beautiful dinner on the table and pour two glasses of
wine. Your partner walks through the door and immediately
begins to complain about something you said a few days before. You become furious and start an argument that ruins
the whole evening.

What do these three experiences have in common beyond ending in unhappiness? In each circumstance you had an expectation of how things would and should transpire. What actually unfolded was diametrically opposed to your expectation. You were unable to accept the difference between reality and your illusion of what that reality should have been. As a result, you reacted with fear, anger or frustration because your ego was bitterly disappointed.

As the former Beatle, singer/songwriter and political activist John Lennon put it in a song for his newborn son, "life is what happens while you're busy making other plans." Most of us are making other plans all the time, and getting stressed out when life happens differently. We are so caught up in our egos and focused on getting what we want that we continuously think we are the central character, director and producer in the Movie of Life, and when it fails to unfold according to our script we experience angst. This often becomes a chronic pattern that creates a stream of anxiety and discontent.

Sutra 2.42 *Santoshad Annuttamah Sukkha Labhah.*

"Through contentment, supreme joy is obtained."

The second of the Niyamas is **Santosha**, or contentment. This is the most elusive of emotions for most of us, and among the most blessed to attain. The key to any lasting contentment is learning to see and accept reality for what it is and then acting skillfully, rather than reacting when reality fails to conform to our expectations. In doing this, we come to recognize there is more going on than just our own little movie, that our ego is not running the world and that there is a higher power behind our experience.

In the sacred yogic text of the Bhagavad-Gita, when Krishna admonishes Arjuna not to be moved by pleasure or pain, he is telling him to stop reacting to adversity, to see reality clearly and to stay detached in the process. Further, Krishna was instructing Arjuna to do what was necessary in life, no matter how challenging or seemingly odious, and to take skillful action rather than simply reacting with despair over his circumstance.

When I was seeking to heal from failed back surgery and terminal cancer, one of the most important turning points involved learning to release despair, face reality, cultivate gratitude and take action as skillfully as I was able. For several years I had been deeply depressed about being crippled and losing my career. This was treated with painkillers and anti-depressants that only served to cloud my soul. I believe this imbalance helped to set the stage for the subsequent cancer, which was then addressed with stronger medications to further mask the symptoms of physical and psychological pain. Seeing myself as a victim only worsened my despair.

Shortly after I detoxified, cold-turkey, from all medications and began my journey into healing, a pain episode began in my lower back. Typically, such an event would last for days and all but paralyze me, even with the strongest drugs in my pharmaceutical arsenal. My usual reaction was to feel anger, fear, self-pity and frustration. This time, I chose to embrace and thank the pain while breathing deeply into it. To my amazement, the pain began to slowly decrease. Within a few hours it was gone. It felt like a miracle.

I began thanking my pain each and every day, thanking the loss of my career, the failed surgery and the cancer. At the same time, I became devoted to all aspects of my Yoga practice, embracing it with full faith as the pathway to my survival. There were still many struggles and periods of great physical pain and emotional turmoil, but I slowly began to get the upper hand. Without being directly aware of it, I was facing reality for the first time in years. I was no longer reacting to my circumstances. Instead, I was seeking to act as skillfully as possible. Had I not made this shift, I do not believe I would be alive today.

One of the primary reasons that most of us spend our lives reacting to reality, and feeling stressed and unhappy as a result, is because we have been deliberately conditioned to do so. The credo of marketing is to create a need and fill it. The intent is to sow the seeds of discontent, making us feel our lives are inadequate. We are then offered a way out of our unhappiness through continuously purchasing goods and services. Our entire economy is based upon this illusion.

Another factor has to do with the constriction of our range. Much of our social conditioning results in increasingly narrow viewpoints and experiences. We come to see the world through our lens of political, social and philosophical prejudices. We seek physical comforts and avoid exertion or exposure to the elements. We live more and more vicariously, finding our own lives mediocre in comparison to those we see glorified in the media. Our tolerance for anything outside of our range is diminished as we become more and more set in our ways. When the inevitable fluctuations of life spike outside of our comfort zone, we react.

This not only occurs on an individual level, but on a national level as well. As a nation becomes more intolerant and set in its ways, it is more likely to have conflict with the world around it. America has a history of becoming angry with

countries that fall outside of its tolerance range and then reacting with aggression towards them. We have engaged in hundreds of foreign military exploits since our nation was founded
and now spend more than half-a-million dollars every minute
on the military. Much of our aggression has only served to
diminish our standing in the world. Surely some of these conflicts were unavoidable and, as in the case of World War Two,
we were responding to a legitimate global threat. But many of
our conflicts have arisen from over-reaction, from a national
ego trying to control the political script for the world.

We cannot change our national mood or foreign policy
overnight, but we can begin to change ourselves. We can
come to understand that we are not the center of the world but
are a part of the oneness of all that is. We are not in control
of reality. In fact, often times we do not even perceive reality
correctly. We must come to see what truly is, rather than focus
on what we feel should be. Instead of always minding what
happens, we must learn to be mindful and then act wisely.

There is an old cliché warning us to be careful of what
we ask for since we might get it. Often times, our desires
will only cause us more suffering if fulfilled. An extreme
example of this is the alarmingly high level of depression
and suicide amongst people who win large sums of money
in the lottery. Their greatest dream seems fulfilled, only to
becomes a nightmare as they realize that money does not
equate with happiness or contentment.

The over-pursuit of pleasure can lead to pain and suffering. We immediately understand this if we eat or drink too
much. Seeking pleasure through over-consumption of material goods can result in the misery of debt. The average
American household has $10,000 in credit card debt and col-

lectively we are more than 60-billion dollars in the hole. Any and every type of over-indulgence inevitably creates imbalance and leads to suffering.

Conversely, situations that we might consider horrible at first blush often turn out to be blessings in disguise. How many of us have despaired over the loss of a job or relationship only to find with time that a better job or more meaningful relationship unfolded? I have come to realize that a broken back and cancer were two of the greatest blessings of my life and continue to be grateful for these experiences. Yet if we are told to have gratitude when we are in the throes of our hopelessness we are likely to angrily reject the suggestion as foolish and insulting.

This is why Krishna urged Arjuna to remain detached. This does not mean to stick our heads in the sand and never enjoy ourselves. When true pleasure arises, we should experience it fully and appreciate it. We should not, however, become attached and blindly seek it out at all costs. When pain and suffering arise, we should embrace the messages they carry, and take appropriate action rather than seek to lash out or run and hide.

Through cultivating gratitude and acceptance we begin to expand our range, live more fully in reality and increase the level of Santosha in our lives. As we accept experience in one area of life and learn to cope with challenges, we are able to expand in other areas. This helps us release our egos, preconceptions and prejudices and move past the boundaries of our social conditioning. This, in turn, promotes fuller expression, a greater willingness to take chances and enhanced self-esteem.

Practicing the Yamas also helps us sow the seeds of contentment. Through Ahimsa, or non-violence, we find peace. We learn to love rather than to harm. We live more from our hearts, with compassion and understanding, instead of with anger and fear.

Through Satya, or truth, we come to see reality more clearly. We face ourselves and our preconceived notions, gaining greater clarity and purpose. We no longer need to remember falsehoods so as to keep our stories straight.

Through Asteya, or non-stealing, we cultivate greater harmony, become mindful of the preciousness of Mother Earth and her resources, and feel a sense of integrity and increased self-esteem.

Through Bramicharya, or non-overindulging, we become less impulsive and compulsive. We realize that gratifying our ego and indulging our senses is a trap. We become more self-contained.

Through Aparigraha, or non-greediness, we learn to be more satisfied with what we have and thankful for the abundance in our lives. We remember the blessing of our breath, the endless gifts of Mother Nature, and the pure joy of simply being alive and having the consciousness to be aware of it.

Once we have sewn these sacred seeds in our hearts, our ongoing cultivation of the Yamas and Niyamas allows the serenity and peace of contentment to germinate, sprout and blossom in our lives.

Practice

As a practice in Santosha, allow thoughts of gratitude and acceptance to ride on the waves of your breath. Breathe in gratitude and let it permeate every cell of your being. Breathe out acceptance and open your heart to all that is, embracing every single aspect of live. After several minutes of this practice, begin to breathe in peace, and when you breathe out, visualize contentment flowing through you like a radiant, golden light.

When aggravations and reactions arise, remind yourself not to mind what happens. Remember that reacting only causes emotional imbalance and contributes nothing towards addressing or solving the situation. Seek to clearly see and accept reality and devise a plan to act with skill.

Become aware of those times when your ego is running the show, when you are succumbing to your social conditioning or falling back into your constricted range. Let go of those old agreements and habituated responses and find your true expression.

Living in Santosha is living from the heart. It is a full blossoming of Yoga and brings a delightful fragrance into our life that helps us to heal ourselves and calm those in our presence. It is also what we all truly want. There is no greater gift than this, no acquisition or experience that can compare, no level of power, wealth or status that even comes close to the grace of true contentment.

*We can study Yoga
and come to know
its myriad aspects and applications,
but we must practice it
with enduring effort
and self-discipline
for it to unfold its many blessings in our lives.*

CHAPTER ELEVEN
Tapas

The birth of a new star, as seen in photos from the Hubble Spacecraft, looks remarkably like the transmutation of a fertilized egg in a woman's womb. A bolt of lightning mirrors the firing of a nerve cell. The branches and stems of a great tree echo a human brain and neurological system. The patterns of a riverbed, with its branching arteries and tributaries, emulate our veins and arteries. The very rhythm of our heartbeat is one with the rhythm of the universe.

More than being pleasing metaphors, these similarities reflect consistencies in the macrocosm and the microcosm. This is Dharma, or Divine Law, and it is universal and immutable. Divine Law permeates and governs all that is. Among the most important aspects of Divine Law is the principle of sustained effort.

For a tree to burst forth from a seed, push through the soil and soar into the sky, a mighty effort is required. For wild animals to migrate, from caribou on the northern plains to Canadian geese to great whales, a mighty effort is required. For an athlete, artist, intellectual or entrepreneur to excel, a mighty effort is required. For all of life to survive and thrive, a mighty effort is required. This is the central principle of Yoga and the very essence of *Tapas*.

Sutra 2.43 *Kayedriya Siddhir Asuddhi Ksayat Tapasah.*

"By austerity, impurities of body and senses are destroyed and occult powers gained."

Yoga is based upon action, as an embodiment and an expression of Vedic wisdom. Tapas is the austerity, hard work, self-discipline and sustained effort it takes to achieve Yoga. We can know everything there is to know about food, from planting to harvesting to serving, but we must ingest it to be nourished. We can study Yoga and come to know its myriad aspects and applications, but we must practice it with enduring effort and self-discipline for it to unfold its many blessings in our lives.

Yoga can be likened to a bellows, and the laws governing both are one and the same. We must make the effort to pick up the bellows and pump it vigorously to ignite and grow a fire. For Yoga to be successful, we must take it up with diligent and devoted effort in order to ignite and sustain the inner fire of healing, growth and transformation. Tapas is the catalyst, without which our potential remains inert.

The root of Tapas is "tap", which means to apply one's heart. Hence, Tapas is also the inner flame of the heart required to burn away our impurities and transform the fuel of knowledge into the elixir of wisdom. We all possess this fire, and it is inherent in all matter, but it is often dormant. Even dried sticks of wood, when vigorously rubbed together over a sustained period of time, will reveal their inner flame. And so it is with each of us.

The Western allopathic and palliative model of medicine we have discussed is the opposite of Tapas. We are led to believe that we can have our cake and eat it too, that we need not take responsibility for our choices or suffer their consequences. We can live out of alignment with Divine Law and treat our ensuing suffering with medications and surgeries, no effort required.

Much of modern, New Age philosophy makes the same false promise of health and prosperity without any effort to achieve these goals. We are led to believe, and often deeply hope, that a psychic, pranic healer, medical intuitive or mystic might make us whole through their touch, wisdom or insight. Others would have us merely visualize our desires, assuring us they will then manifest as the energy of the universe aligns with our intention.

Religion often makes the same promise, as do some Yoga gurus and other spiritual leaders who would have us join their flock to receive *shaktipat*, or spiritual energy, through their presence and touch. Through any method of seeking effortless, external solutions and saviors for our internal problems, we delude ourselves and surrender our power and the true ability to heal. While we can be deeply inspired by a sermon, energized by a guru or moved by a New Age practitioner, any positive effect will be temporary unless we add the catalyst of Tapas.

The same principle applies when we tune into mass media. We seek emotional experience through the drama and comedy of movies and television programming, or excitement and adventure through sports, documentaries and travelogues. But it is all vicarious and ultimately fruitless, like watching someone else lift weights in hopes of building our own biceps. Through this process of substituting artificial and effortless distraction for true experience, we surrender not only our power, but our consciousness as well.

Through Tapas we take full responsibility for our healing and our spiritual growth. It implies a complete commitment, and it demands we expend the necessary energy to fulfill that commitment. To align ourselves with Divine Law we must move into right diet, right exercise, right thinking and right lifestyle. We must also move from passivity to positive action. This requires breaking old habits and extracting ourselves from the bubble of social conditioning, which can only be accomplished with great and consistent effort.

Through Tapas we also reclaim our power. We affirm our inherent ability to overcome, achieve and transform our lives rather than surrendering to the false hope of effortless, external salvation. When we deny this power we deny our dignity as Divine Beings, and render ourselves vulnerable and adrift. Tapas, therefore, is an inner revolution and reclamation of our Souls.

Tapas is also essential to Ayurveda. We heal through taking responsibility for, and charge of, our lives. This is done through realigning ourselves with Divine Law and harmonizing ourselves with the rhythms of Mother Nature. Just as we must dig ditches for water to irrigate our crops, so must we pierce through the crust of our resistance and establish daily practices and rituals to embrace mindful and balanced living.

The Yoga Sutras warn us about the five Kleshas, discussed in Chapter Five, of ignorance, ego, attraction, aversion and fear. Patanjali also lists the five types of mental activity.

Sutra 1:6 *Pramana Viparyaya Vikalpa Nidra Smrta.*

"They are right knowledge, false knowledge, verbal delusion, sleep and memory."

Pramana, or right knowledge, comes through direct perception, actually experiencing something and understanding it through that experience. As a fundamental example, we can warn a child endlessly about touching a hot stove, but the lesson is truly learned and retained if the child touches the stove and screams with pain. After that direct experience, we need never remind them again.

Viparyaya, or false knowledge, involves delusion, illusion or hallucination. The oft-used story in yogic literature illustrating false knowledge is of a man who sees a coiled rope in the dark of night and mistakes it as a snake. He runs through the village warning all he can find and is ultimately humiliated when he brings his fellows out in the dark to slay the rope.

Vikalpa, or imagination, is wishful thinking with no basis in fact. It typically arises from our ingrained misperceptions, petty desires and need to rationalize the ego.

Nidra, or sleep, is our state of mind without any perception. Experiences, memories and thought patterns arise and fall in distorted form and leave us in complete ignorance if we embrace them as real.

Smriti, or memory, is a valuable source and usually arises from right knowledge, but can be based upon false or wishful recollections. We might recall dreams, misperceptions and illusions and mistake them as valid memories.

Of the five, of course, right knowledge through direct perception is superior. Ayurveda recognizes three means of obtaining right knowledge. They are *Pratyaksha*, or direct perception, *Anumana*, or inference, and *Aptopadesha*, or instruction. We can learn much through inference, recognizing that where there is smoke there is likely to be fire. Knowledge comes to us through authentic teaching as well, but we must ensure the integrity of the information. These three means to right knowledge are valuable, but again, direct perception reigns.

The essence of Yoga and Ayurveda is the development of our own direct perception, so that we have an immediate experience of the creative and transformative processes of life. The key to this direct perception is Tapas. We must expend the energy to have the experience and extract the knowledge and wisdom that arises from it. Tapas ignites the light in our hearts and expresses itself as courage, commitment, discipline, self-reliance and inner strength. It is the purest form of holistic medicine that propels us forward on our journey. Without Tapas we are fooling ourselves in any quest for healing or spiritual evolution.

We can liken Tapas to the alchemy of purifying gold. In order to obtain the precious metal, we must first heat it to the melting point so that all impurities are burned away. Through Tapas, we stoke our inner fire and burn away our obstacles and impurities, finding the precious metal of our true selves in the process. We arise from the ashes of this process, like the phoenix, as transformed beings.

At the heart of Tapas is daily practice. Through the power of daily practice we re-habituate ourselves and align with our highest aspirations. Patanjali speaks to the power of daily practice while discussing the ultimate goal of Yoga: merging with the Divine.

Sutra 1:21: *Tivra Samveganam Asannah.*

"To the keen and intent practitioner this comes very quickly."

Sutra 1:22: *Mrdu Madhyadhimatratvat Tatopi Visehah.*

"The time necessary for success further depends upon whether

the practice is mild, medium or intense."

In other words, the greater our commitment, as expressed through the Tapas of our daily practice, the greater the results. Many of us, despite what we might say, do not want to heal. We find a dark comfort in our hurts, dramas and resentments. We hold onto our physical pain and disease as a way of masking our fear of failure. We cling to self-pity as a means of seeking attention and as an excuse for not being all that we truly could be. Our level of Tapas, which determines the intensity of the inner fire needed to burn away our suffering, reveals the true level of our desire to heal.

When I was taking heavy medications for cancer and back pain I spoke often of my desire to heal but made no real effort to do so. I had fully surrendered to my disease and disability. My self-pity provided a deranged sense of comfort. I expected others to treat me as someone who, as a result of my suffering, deserved their special consideration and care. During this time, which spanned several years, I did not have a true desire to heal. I lacked integrity, dignity and courage. I made no effort, and this left me with no inner fire. Deep down I wanted to disappear, and I was in the process of doing so as the cancer was claiming my life.

When my little boy implored me to "get up, daddy!" it was as if the universe itself was shaking me awake. As a result of this shift, I tapped into the power of Tapas. I was fortunate to have saved enough during my journalism career to sustain myself through several years of intense daily practice. I often began at 3 in the morning and ended after sunset, only taking time out from studies and practices in Yoga and Ayurveda to be with my son. Through this direct experience and devoted effort I not only healed, I reclaimed my power, my dignity, my consciousness and my very Soul.

I came to realize through this process that I was no one special and my healing was not miraculous. We all possess an incredible inner power to heal and evolve; unfortunately, it is a power from which we have been largely disenfranchised. Yoga is the process of reclaiming this power and Tapas is the key ingredient, the very essence of taking skillful action.

Practice

Never allow anyone to tell you that you do not have the ability to persevere in your efforts. Especially, never allow that critic within you to deny your power and ability. You are a Divine Being with infinite capability. The power of your body, mind and Soul is limitless. Despite all obstacles, struggles and perceived shortcomings, at your very core you are the brightest of flames and purest of gold. Embrace Tapas and the precious radiance of your Being will burst forth and light the world.

This said, do not try to do too much at once. This is a recipe for becoming overwhelmed and feeling like a failure. Identify one or two things that you have long wished to change in your life that are fairly simple and most achievable given the circumstances of your life. It is often best to start with the body then move to aspects of your lifestyle and outlook that also need attention. Review your diet and note if there are things crying out for change. Address them one or two at a time. A simple gesture, such as quitting coffee or a particular junk food, can affirm your ability to take charge and implement change.

Establishing or recommitting to a short daily Yoga practice, or sadhana, is also essential to Tapas. This can involve a few Yoga poses, some breath awareness and a simple meditation.

10-15 minutes every morning is enough to help you create a shift in your life and empower you to move forward and expand from there. You will find many suggestions in this regard in the Appendix of Practices.

The key is to sustain your progress, take further steps only when you are ready, and to have undying faith that you possess great power and ability to become the master of your life and unfold your fullest potential.

*While we have become more intimate
with distant galaxies
and the inner workings of the
smallest of living cells,
we have made little collective headway
in exploring the
vast frontier of consciousness
within us.*

CHAPTER TWELVE
Svadhyaya

The opposite of perpetually seeking to escape ourselves through distraction and external stimuli is the journey of finding ourselves, of looking deeply within to discover who we truly are and what the ultimate purpose of our lives might be. This questioning has been at the core of spiritual practice for all time. It is, in many ways, a never-ending quest.

Humankind has explored every corner of the Earth. We have propelled ourselves into space, created amazingly powerful telescopes to look beyond our reach, and engineered equally powerful microscopes to peer into the depths of matter. While we have become more intimate with distant galaxies and the inner workings of the smallest of living cells, we have made little collective headway in exploring the vast frontier of consciousness within us.

The process of cultivating this self-awareness is *Svadhyaya*.

Sutra 2.44 *Svadhyayad Istadevata Samprayogah.*

"Through self-study and reflection on sacred words one unifies with one's chosen deity."

Svadhyaya, or self-study and reflection on sacred words, is a primary pathway to self-awareness and personal growth. Practicing the Yamas assists us in this regard, for as we see our own challenges and habituated ways, we learn more about who we are and where we need healing and change.

Svadhyaya also helps move us past the Kleshas – ignorance of our true nature, ego, attraction, aversion and fear. It involves facing ourselves and really owning our behavior, then seeking the guidance embodied in sacred words that offers us a higher course of action and being.

In unifying with one's chosen deity, noted in the above sutra, we are actually unifying with the Divine. The many deities of Yoga, such as Shiva, Krishna, Rama and Vishnu, are personifications of the forces of the Divine. We can call this ultimate being Brahma or God, our Higher Power or Nature. We can look to Christ, Buddha or Mohammed, Mary Magdalene or Kali. Whether historic figures or archetypes, all are aspects of our own nature, all inspirational embodiments or symbols of eternal consciousness and pure awareness. In bringing our attention to our own personal or chosen deity, or *Ishta Devata*, we are accessing our own divinity.

Reflecting on sacred words primarily means studying sacred texts. In yogic practice these texts include the Vedas, Bhagavad-Gita, Yoga Sutras, and Upanishads. Depending upon our spiritual orientation, we can look to the Bible, Qur'an, the Diamond Sutra of Buddhism, the Tao Te Ching or any other truly sacred text containing spiritual wisdom. This scriptural studying helps us study ourselves as well. In reading and rereading this wisdom, we come to see our perspectives and patterns in a different light. We have communication with those great sages and seers who have actually explored the inner frontier and brought home divine guidance. We are inspired to shift, change and grow. Our hearts are opened and our souls are touched.

Consider this excerpt from the Upanishads:

"When all the desires that surge in the heart
Are renounced, the mortal becomes immortal.
When all the knots that strangle the heart
Are loosened, the mortal becomes immortal,
Here in this very life.
Even as a mirror stained by dust
Shines brilliantly when it has been cleansed,
So the embodied one, on seeing the nature of the Soul,
Becomes unitary, his end attained, from sorrow freed."

The more we study and contemplate such writings, which are the very essence of inner awareness, the more we are inspired and supported on our journey. Each of us is an incredibly complex emotional being. We have all of the grace of the Divine within us, and we have all of the lower instincts of existence as well. We have the capacity to be angelic or wicked, peaceful or violent, compassionate or self-absorbed. Svadhyaya guides us into knowing and honoring our higher Self. Through this process we awaken to the greater meaning of life and move away from the more base and negative aspects of our being.

In this process, not only do we further extract ourselves from the bubble of social conditioning, we also come face to face with ourselves. To move past a negative behavior pattern, we must first recognize it. Then we must own it. We must give up the excuses and rationales, the pointing of fingers at others or at external circumstances, and accept that our lower nature has been prevailing. Only then can we begin the process of releasing it and building more conscious attitudes and actions.

After healing from cancer and a broken back, I came to realize there was much more work to be done. Through the constant pain, medications and depression, I had allowed my lower nature to thrive. While embracing my new path, I still felt anger, fear and frustration. I struggled with feeling like a victim and letting go of the past and all of its hurts. But eventually, through Svadhyaya, I cleansed the dust from my mirror, stared myself straight in the eyes, owned up to my problems and slowly untied the knots strangling my heart. As promised in the Upanishads, I was freed from much of my self-created suffering and sorrow.

As my practice deepened, I came to understand that there was something much greater than my individual story. Despite its life-threatening magnitude, it was only a story when I was sick and dying, and only a story when I experienced the grace of healing. And while any such narrative can illustrate the positive benefits of taking charge of one's life and is therefore worth retelling, clinging to it inhibits a full healing. Through the self-inquiry of Svadhyaya we actually move away from our self-story and are reminded of the larger picture and the eternal nature of existence.

This, too, provides a release from the ego. To find our true Self, we must transcend our small self. To merge with the Divine, we must leave our "stuff" behind, or at least put it into its proper place as the small change it actually is. Sacred texts guide and inspire us in this process, providing the wisdom of our greatest seers and sages.

"The self-controlled soul, who moves amongst sense objects, free from either attachment or repulsion, he wins eternal Peace." **Krishna**

"All that we are is the result of what we have thought. If a man speaks or acts with an evil thought, pain follows him. If a man speaks or acts with a pure thought, happiness follows him, like a shadow that never leaves him." **Buddha**

"Ask and it will be given to you; seek and you will find; knock and the door will be opened to you." **Jesus Christ**

We would benefit from the self-study of Svadhyaya as a nation as well. America has become deeply unpopular around the world. We are seen by many as aggressive, bullying, exploitative and self-centered. This pervasive animosity towards us holds many messages. We can choose as a people to heap scorn upon those who dare to criticize us, point out their faults and become their enemies, or we can use these negative perceptions of us as a mirror that is reflecting an aspect of our behavior that bears scrutiny and contemplation.

Americans also have done many great things for the world. We have helped rebuild nations after devastating wars, established global charities to combat major diseases, starvation and poverty, and opened our country to millions of immigrants escaping oppression and injustice. This is living from the heart. We also have decimated the indigenous people of America, exploited Africans as slaves, fomented racism and prejudice, used too much of the world's resources, polluted Mother Earth and waged unjust wars. This is living from the ego.

National reflection of this sort may be too idealistic or too far off given our collective consciousness at present, but the process begins with each of us as individuals. It includes recognizing that our personal deities, or Ista Devatas, or our decision to embrace many or none at all, is not the issue.

There is no one exclusive savior, no single path with an exclusive grip on the truth that makes all other paths suspect and sacrilegious. This is a reversion to ego and promotes further conflict, misunderstanding and alienation. The issue is to find our true selves, to embrace a path and, through the power of Tapas, stay with it until we arrive at a point of clearer understanding of who we are and what reality is. As with all spiritual practice, this shift of awareness comes with the doing. Not only must we explore the sacred texts and knowledge of our chosen path, we must then turn this knowledge into wisdom by actually bringing it into our lives and living it. This is the very essence of Sadhana, of true spiritual practice. It is a journey into bliss, a finding of the true paradise that has always existed within us. It is also a challenge, especially in a modern world in which we are constantly drawn away from the practice by powerful and seemingly omnipresent forces.

Patanjali offers us some tools to sustain ourselves, including *Sraddha, Virya, Prajna* and *Smriti*. Sraddha is faith, a conviction that our commitment to our journey will bear fruit in its own time as long as we remain patient, devoted and steady. Virya is courage, finding the inner strength to move forward, to extract ourselves from the bubble of our conditioning and to release our fear and insecurities. Prajna is the flashes of insight and wisdom that arise from our practice. Smriti is memory, a holding onto the Prajna, especially when we face doubt, tumult and resistance.

Yoga holds that our deepest and truest consciousness dwells in our hearts, not our brains. The mind in our head, although incredibly necessary and useful, is externally oriented and tied to our senses. The mind in the heart holds the eternal wisdom of our souls. Svadhyaya moves us towards hearing this deeper voice and accessing its intelligence and guidance. This is the Yoga of Living from the Heart.

Practice

As a practice, choose your source of spiritual wisdom and commit to fully exploring it. In the Vedic tradition, as mentioned, the Yoga Sutras, Bhagavad-Gita and Upanishads offer a wealth of insight, inspiration and guidance. Don't try to read or memorize it all. Instead, pick one text, perhaps even revisiting a text with which you are already familiar, and be with it for 10-15 minutes each day. Let the sages speak to your heart, allow the wisdom to percolate and sink in.

Contemplate what your story is. See it as just that, a story. Look to ways you can move beyond it and find a higher truth. Look to your heart for guidance instead of always allowing the mind to run amok. When old patterns of awareness arise, don't buy into them this time. Journal your insights and experiences of Svadhyaya. Through faith, courage, flashes of insight and memory, move forward in a slow and steady fashion and welcome this new Self into your life with open arms.

When we remember
how sacred it is to be alive,
the blessing of our breath,
the water we drink,
the food we eat,
the breeze on our faces
and the song of birds in flight,
we are sensing the Divine.

CHAPTER THIRTEEN
Ishvara Pranidhana

The mantra *Aham Brahmasmi,* "I and Brahman are one," is at the core of Vedantic Self-realization. Brahman is the Supreme Cosmic Spirit, an abstract awareness of God. *Ishvara* is also this Supreme Being, in a more personal and tangible sense. While there are many different schools of thought on this aspect of yogic spirituality, and some academic debate as to precise meanings and definitions, the point is that we are Divine Beings, individuated drops of the eternal ocean of Supreme Consciousness that animates all that is.

Knowing or studying this concept provides the grist of spiritual intellectualism. But knowing alone is not enough. Actually experiencing it, merging with the Divine within us and seeing it in all creation, is true spiritual awareness, an attainment of the very highest form of Self-realization. This is the ultimate Vidya, or wisdom, and the ultimate aim of Yoga.

Sutra II:45 *Samadhi Siddhir Ishvarapranhidanat.*

"By total surrender to God, Samadhi is attained."

Samadhi is the eighth and final limb of Patanjali's Ashtanga system and will be explored in greater detail in Chapter Nineteen. It involves absorption, or unification, with the object of our meditation, a true merging that brings us towards a pure state of enlightenment. Patanjali is telling us that simply through Ishvara Pranidhana, seeing the Divine in all things, we can get there. This is the central principle of Bhakti Yoga, the Yoga of Devotion.

The very first of the Five Kleshas, or afflictions discussed earlier as the causes of our suffering, is Avidya. This means, again, lack of wisdom (Vidya), or ignorance. It means that we have forgotten who we truly are. We have forgotten that we are Divine. This leads us into our egos, likes, dislikes, fears and the inevitable suffering they create for us. Ishvara Pranidhana is the act of constantly remembering who we are, and it offers a pathway out of this suffering.

Patanjali also notes that Ishvara is the Supreme Purusha, the ultimate Self, as differentiated from Prakriti, or nature, which is ever-changing and unstable. Ishvara, he tells us, is all knowledge, the wisdom of all times, the teacher of all teachers. Each of us has this wisdom within us. It is muted, however, by our frantic minds and lifestyles of distraction and desire. In this distracted state we become identified with Prakriti, with the fluctuations of nature and the material world. We think we are our bodies and our minds, we forget that the eternal Purusha even exists, much less dwells within us.

When we enter Yoga and practice stilling the mind and cultivating inner awareness, we begin to access our internal wisdom. This is how the great sages downloaded the profound spiritual teachings of the Vedas. They sat in extended meditation and opened to the Divine Intelligence within. We can see throughout history that this very same wisdom, albeit articulated in a variety of languages and shaped by a multiplicity of cultures, has been accessed by saints and sages of all theologies and lies at the core of all true religious teachings.

When we remember how sacred it is to be alive, the blessing of our breath, the water we drink, the food we eat, the breeze on our faces and the song of birds in flight, we are sensing the Divine. We come to understand that we are part of something much bigger than our individuated selves, that we belong to something much greater. We begin to see the macrocosm in the microcosm, each thread in the fabric of life part of the tapestry of the cosmos.

Ishvara Pranidhana also means fully surrendering to the Divine and seeing the Divine in all things. This, ultimately, is a full surrender of the ego. While we might find it easy to see the grace within those we love, it is deeper work to see the Divine in those with whom we disagree or feel enmity towards. This is at the core of forgiveness, compassion, acceptance and understanding. We can easily go to war with an enemy whose actions, beliefs and lifestyle we can dismiss, vilify and condemn. When we see them as our brothers and sisters, woven as we are in the multicolored mosaic of humankind, we must naturally reassess our position, face our prejudices and seek healing rather than conflict.

The Divine is not only within us, it inhabits all living things. It permeates the water and wind, the mountains and valleys, the moon and stars, the tiniest grain of sand and the greatest of galaxies. Yet while it is everywhere, the only place we find it is in the present moment. With our fixations on the past and future, our chronic comings and goings, our mental scenarios and hypothesizing, the present moment is elusive. Stillness and silence have become strangers to us. We ever wonder, "What is next?" We scurry here and there, rarely fully focused on what we are doing, but instead focusing on what is coming next. In missing the moment, we disconnect from the Divine. We forget. We suffer.

If you put this book down right now, you can reconnect.

Go outside and gaze into the sky, feel the breeze caress your cheeks, notice the subtle sounds of nature, connect with any trees and plants around you. Remember that the Divine is within all that you are experiencing, and feel it within you. This is Ishvara Pranidhana, this is coming home to the never-ending stream of the present moment, to the true and only reality that ever has been or ever shall be. In this sacred moment, everything is as it should be, everything is perfect—every single thing, including you.

Children are masters of this practice. They are the true inhabitants of the moment, although social conditioning pulls them away from this grace too quickly. One of my most profound experiences of this was one night long after sunset when I was preparing my then 4-year old boy for bed. He was curled up in my arms, warm and snug in his pajamas, when he looked up at me and whispered, "Daddy, before bed, let's go sit on the front porch and listen to the dark."

We went and sat on our Cape Cod porch bench in the evening silence and listened to the dark. The Divine embraced us as we effortlessly merged into the grace of it all. So simple, so silent, so sacred. All we need to do is to stop, listen, look and be. It is not listening to distracting noises or looking at specific objects, it is a sensory awareness of timelessness, the presence of eternity within and without. It is merging with the purest of consciousness, listening to the dark, allowing the whisper of life to speak directly to our souls.

Sutra I:27 *Tasya Vacakah Pranava.*

"The word that expresses Ishvara is the mystic sound of OM."

OM is the ultimate mantra, the sound of the universe, the

name of the Divine. There is a resonance in each of the 70-plus trillion cells in our bodies and throughout the entire universe, a song sung by each whirling galaxy in the cosmos. It is there in the denseness of rocks and the lightness of the air. It is whispered in different pitches and tones, but it is ever the same. This resonance is the sound of OM. This is why we chant OM at the beginning and end of Asana classes, and why OM begins and ends all mantras. The mere chanting of this sacred sound is a practice of Ishvara Pranidhana.

Through OM we retune our inner rhythm, we reconnect with the cosmos, we express and embody the vibration of the sacredness of all being. The humming sound of OM is called *Pranava* because it is connected to our Prana, or life force. Its repetition is among the highest forms of Vedic spiritual meditation and is central to all Vedic spiritual texts. Also written as AUM, this sacred mantra embodies Brahma, Vishnu and Shiva, the powers of creation, preservation and destruction. It is said that all speech and all consciousness arises from OM/AUM. As Patanjali reminds us, it is the sound of Ishvara, the very voice of the Divine.

Together, the last three Niyamas of Tapas, Svadhyaya and Ishvara Pranidhana constitute what Patanjali calls Kriya Yoga, the Yoga of Action. He tells us in the very first Sutra of the second Pada, which is dedicated to Sadhana (practice), that disciplined and dedicated practice, self-inquiry through study of spiritual texts and constant awareness of, and devotion to, the Divine are necessary actions for achieving Yoga. This is the process of taking charge of our lives, moving from the mundane to the spiritual, and finding our higher truth in life.

As the last of the Niyamas, or personal observances, Ishvara Pranidhana asks us to surrender to the Divine in all that we do. This means making our best effort in each and every moment to be aware, to be present, mindful and conscious of this ultimate reality. This practice also strengthens our observances of all the Yamas and Niyamas. When we are aware of the Divine nature of existence, it is easier to embrace the essence of non-harming, truthfulness, non-stealing, continence and non-possessiveness. It becomes intuitive that ingesting mental or physical toxins through junk impressions or junk food dishonors the divinity of our minds and bodies. Contentment is less elusive as we release the ego and a constricted, controlling view of the world. We can more readily embrace our inner power and find the strength, determination and commitment to further our journey. We come to know our true selves with greater insight and clarity.

As we sustain this awareness to the best of our abilities, its power begins to shine forth. We find that compassion and humility replace judgment and arrogance; gratitude and acceptance take the place of selfishness and resistance; love and peace rise above hatred and harming. This is living from the heart in the sacred truth of Yoga.

Practice

To practice Ishvara Pranidhana, begin in your home. Make it the most sacred space possible. Creating an altar is a reminder of the Divine. It can be small and simple or spacious and elaborate. Stones, crystals, candles and water are reminders of the elements. If you have an Ista Devata, or chosen deity, a picture or statue can be powerful. Your altar should have a prominent place in your home and be well tended to, kept clean and visited often. The simple act of lighting a candle at our altar reminds us of Ishvara, of the light of consciousness that dwells within our hearts.

Become more aware of the seasons. Spend more time in nature and deeply notice the plants and animals, the earth and sky, the wind and water. Connect with the sacredness of all manifestations of nature, from the tiniest insect to a beautiful bird or a mighty tree reaching to the heavens. See Spirit everywhere. As you do, feel profound gratitude for the water you drink, the food you eat, the earth upon which you walk and the air you breathe.

Chant OM often, especially during your practice or at your altar. You might also use the silent inner mantra of Aham Brahmasmi, remembering that you and Brahman are one, or So Ham, meaning simply "I am." Let yourself become more and more aware of the present moment and move beyond thoughts of the past and future. See the Divine in all that is.

*Through Asana
we not only release physical toxins,
we actually squeeze out,
untie and release
emotional knots and blockages
stored in our tissues and organs.
When we stretch ourselves
beyond our constricted limitations,
we cultivate the
fire of self-discipline
and personal transformation.*

CHAPTER FOURTEEN
Asana

Most Americans see Yoga as a form of exercise, a "stretch and sweat" routine that enhances flexibility, builds strength and, when therapeutically applied, helps heal back injuries and other physical aches and pains. These poses have been mistaken in the West as being Yoga itself. When we go to class we often say "I'm going to Yoga," but in truth one cannot "go to Yoga." One can only experience Yoga, which arises as a result of dedicated and sustained practice, or Sadhana. Yoga is the higher state of unity, consciousness, harmony and balance with cosmic forces that ultimately arises as a result of our Sadhana.

What we actually "go to" is the Third Limb of Raja Yoga: *Asana*. Asana means posture or seat. The traditional function of Asana is the taking of a seat, cross-legged on the ground, for introspection and meditation. It is an act of holding still, being silent and looking within. The much more popular and modern function of Asana involves the many poses and flowing sequences performed in the Asana classes that are commonly referred to as Yoga classes. Asana is only one component of Yoga and also serves as a therapeutic tool of Ayurveda. This said, however, Asana is an essential and powerful element of the yogic journey and serves as a primary passageway into Yoga.

In the Yoga Sutras, Pantanjali refers very little to Asana, and always refers to it in the context of its meditative function.

Sutra 2.46 *Sthira Sukham Asanam.*

"Asana is a steady, comfortable posture."

Sutra 2.47 *Prayatna Saithily Ananta Samapattibhyam.*

"By lessening the tendency for restlessness and meditating on the Infinite, posture is mastered."

Sutra 2.38 *Tato Dvandva Anabhigatah.*

"Thereafter one is undisturbed by the dualities."

Patanjali is telling us that being able to sit with *Sthira,* or steadiness, and *Sukkha,* or comfort without fidgeting, is Asana. This Sutra also implies a steady and comfortable mind, so that we are not sitting in mental agitation with endless thoughts running through our heads. This is why, traditionally, before even this simple seated meditative pose was practiced, disciples were expected to be well versed in the precepts and observances of the Yamas and Niyamas, and doing their best to live by them. It is easier to sit, merge with the present moment and cultivate higher consciousness when we have purified our bodies and minds, released our egos, and are living in a constant awareness of the Divine. Ayurveda was also a precursor to the spiritual experience of Yoga, as this holistic system of wellness is designed to bring us into greater harmony and balance.

While it would not be practical in our culture to live the Yamas and Niyamas prior to entering an Asana class, it makes perfect sense to do our best to cultivate balanced and ethical living before doing Yoga poses, Pranayama or meditation. We cannot really hold still or come into the present moment, much less cultivate an authentic awareness of the

Divine, if our minds are spinning and our bodies are filled with toxins. We actually run the risk of driving toxins more deeply within our organs and tissues, and further aggravating and energizing the imbalances of our minds, if we seek to practice in such an imbalanced state.

The good news is that practicing Asana contributes greatly to the process of purifying our minds and bodies. Through Asana we not only release physical toxins, we actually squeeze out, untie and release emotional knots and blockages stored in our tissues and organs. When we stretch ourselves beyond our constricted limitations, we cultivate the fire of self-discipline and personal transformation.

Mastering a headstand, finally reaching our toes in a forward fold, or holding a challenging balance pose empowers us. It is tangible proof of our ability to take charge of ourselves and create positive change. Through Asana we access our inner power and build self-reliance. We can then apply this to the circumstances and challenges of our lives off our mats. This helps us cultivate contentment, purity, self-awareness and other aspects of the Yamas and Niyamas.

Sthira and Sukkha, or steadiness and comfort, in Asana also means that in shifting from constriction to suppleness we do not surrender the strength, discipline and effort essential for personal growth. This is embodied in the word Sthira, which also suggests that when our thigh begins to burn in a certain pose, or our hamstring is deeply stretched, we stay in it, we access steadiness through our inner strength and find Sukkha, both physical and mental comfort despite the challenge.

The body and the mind are not actually separate, but are the gross and subtle manifestations of our singular existence. They effect and reflect one another in reciprocal ways. For instance, negative thoughts about the wellness of our physical body can actually lead to imbalance and disease, which is why hypochondriacs tend to get sick. Conversely, not taking care of our bodies often leads to mental imbalances as our self-esteem is diminished and we agonize over our appearance and level of fitness.

If we are tight and constricted in our joints and muscles it is likely that we are also mentally tight. This usually manifests as chronic stress, anger, fear and judgment. If we are supple, limber and fluid in the physical body it is more likely that we will reflect this openness in our mental body. This leads us to creativity, compassion, acceptance, gratitude and an ability to embrace and implement change in our lives. It widens our range, allowing us to be more supple and flexible in life, to face the exigencies of reality with skill instead of anxious reaction when circumstances fail to conform to our expectations.

On a collective level militarism, fundamentalism and rigid social viewpoints all reflect constriction, or a lack of suppleness and acceptance. They lead us to believe that there is only one way of being and doing, and that those who do not believe and do in the same fashion are opponents and enemies. This rigidity leads to misunderstanding and eventually to conflict. Our world has a long history of racism, exploitation, conflict and war that arises from such myopic and self-centered thinking. Peace, on the other hand, arises from a collective mind that is relaxed and open, supple and fluid, accepting of diverse viewpoints and lifestyles, and willing to embrace change and growth.

Practicing Sthira and Sukkha is not only the art of finding steadiness and comfort in a Yoga pose, it is finding these qualities in our lives, especially during moments of greatest challenge. This involves surrendering into what is, accepting rather than resisting, finding our inner strength and inner peace in the most difficult of circumstances. If we force ourselves deeper into a challenging Yoga pose we will likely sustain an injury. If we surrender into it, however, we pave the way for healing and growth. This very same law holds true in relationships. Try to force an issue with your beloved and you are likely to create injury. Surrender into the circumstance and you are likely to experience healing.

Asana, therefore, should never be practiced from the ego, but instead should facilitate a letting go of the ego. If we are comparing ourselves to others in class, seeking to perform the best pose for others to see or pushing too hard to advance our pose, we are in our egos and far from Yoga. When we live our lives from our egos, we are lost in the Kleshas of aversion, attachment and fear. We have forgotten who we truly are, and suffering is inevitable.

Asana also demands that we pay attention. We must feel our bodies to balance them and sense our alignment to open in a pose without pushing into injury. This creates awareness, which brings us into the present moment and away from the past and future where the ego mind typically dwells. Entering into the present moment, as we will explore in the last several limbs of Patanjali's Raja Yoga, is essential to releasing the ego and reaching a state of pure awareness. It is only in this state that we come to understand reality as it truly is, hear the deeper wisdom of our souls, and find the contentment and inner peace that is so elusive in our lives.

While Asana offers all of these benefits and more, we should not solely rely upon it for our experience of Yoga. Asana alone does not counteract an imbalanced life. It does not bring us fully into a merging with higher consciousness. Without the practice of the other limbs of Yoga, it lacks the synergistic power to facilitate lasting transformation and personal growth. Only through bringing the depth of Yogic practice into that far greater portion of our lives when we are not on our mats do we begin to truly nourish and heal all levels of body, mind and soul.

The Asana classes or routines that we choose for ourselves should contribute to greater harmony in our minds and bodies. Through the Ayurvedic system of the **Doshas** we get a deeper understanding of our individual constitution and our imbalances. The three Doshas, *Vata, Pitta* and *Kapha,* are associated, respectively, with air, fire and water. Imbalanced Vata types tend to be ungrounded, prone to worry and anxiety, uncertain and indecisive. Imbalanced Pitta types tend towards anger, being controlling and overly competitive. Imbalanced Kapha types tend to be lethargic, unmotivated and possessive. Each will be drawn to styles of Asana that actually feed their imbalance.

Vatas will seek out flowing Vinayasa style classes with lots of movement and constant change. Pittas will gravitate towards power Yoga and physically challenging classes with an unspoken atmosphere of competition. Kaphas will be drawn to restorative classes with blankets and bolsters and lots of rest. An astute Ayurvedic counselor would put most of the Pittas in the restorative classes to help them relax, the Vatas in the classes with long and powerful holds to build inner strength and ground them, and the Kaphas in a mixture of Vinayasa and powerful classes to get them moving. Doing almost any Asana is far better than doing none at all, but as we become more refined in our practice this Ayurvedic alignment is essential.

My personal experience with Asana was life changing and a central reason that I am alive today. With a broken back, failed surgery and terminal cancer, I was deeply constricted in my body. In a state of depression from losing my career and my health, I was deeply constricted in my mind. With all of the heavy medications I was prescribed, I was deeply removed from any sense of my soul. Asana helped me to detoxify on all of these levels and gain confidence, clarity and healing. It replaced my physical and mental weakness with strength and confidence. It allowed me to see that, despite illness and pain, I could take charge and change my circumstances.

Along with Ayurveda and the pursuit, with various degrees of success, of all the limbs of Yoga, I was able to take my weight down from borderline obesity at 225 pounds to 145 pounds before building myself back up to 160. I practiced many hours every day for several years before scaling back a bit, which also helped me release physical and mental toxins and was central to overcoming cancer. Asana helped me release anxiety, fear, anger, frustration and other negative emotions and attitudes. I have subsequently seen many clients overcome great physical and mental challenges through a devoted Asana routine combined with the Eight Limbs and Ayurvedic modalities.

Through this synergy, we build our vital essences of Prana, Tejas and Ojas. These are the subtle, positive essences behind the imbalances of the Doshas. Prana is our life force and associated with Vata. Tejas is our inner fire, associated with Pitta, and Ojas is our reserve of energy, associated with Kapha. We can see these in the metaphor of a lighted candle. The Ojas is the wax, which is necessary to sustain the flame. The Tejas is the flame itself, while Prana is the radiance of that flame as it shines forth. Yogic practice builds all three and gives us vibrancy, clarity and grace.

Practice

As a practice, determine or review your Dosha (a simple Dosha test can be found in the Appendix). Note if your current Asana practice is likely to help balance or aggravate your Dosha.

If you are Vata, seek to ground yourself in your practice. Try classes that focus on stillness and holding poses. In the flow classes that you love, try to find moments of stillness and grounding and focus upon them. At home, seek Sthira in your practice. In your life off the mat, seek to be more decisive and less worried about outcomes.

If you are Pitta, look for ways to ease off a bit. Exert yourself at only 70-80% of your capacity in the powerful classes you likely love. Do more restorative poses at home and try a few restful classes. Then, review your life off the mat and see if anger, control and judgment are issues for you. If so, work on Ishvara Pranidhana and releasing the ego. Focus on Sukkha.

If you are Kapha, find ways to energize your practice. Take more physically challenging classes, always being mindful of not pushing yourself too far so as to avoid injury. Move your body more with Asana and rest less. Off the mat, seek to be more active, less inclined towards accumulating things, and avoid sedentary habits. You inherently have Sthira and Sukkha, so seek challenge and exertion.

No matter what your Dosha, remember that Asana is a beautiful, powerful, transformative aspect of Yogic practice and not Yoga itself. Ultimately, Yoga asks us to transcend the body as well as the mind and the ego, to be detached, to be in the world but not of it, to ever remember the oneness of all that is. Thus, as Patanjali teaches us, the deepest function of Asana is providing us the ability to hold still, be silent, release the ego and merge with our true nature.

Our breath is a sacred gift.
It is an exchange between
the outer world
and our inner world.
Each inhale we take is a
precious drink of life,
an individuation of the eternal life force.
Every exhale is a
merging back into the eternal.

CHAPTER FIFTEEN
Pranayama

Prana is much more than our breath or personal energy. It is the vital, primal life force that dwells within each of us. It is the light of consciousness that not only animates all human beings, but all living things. It permeates both the microcosm and macrocosm. There are some 70 trillion cells in our bodies. Each is vibrating and pulsating with Prana. Prana is also the sum total of all energy manifest in the universe. Magnetism, heat, light, fossil fuels and electricity are forms of Prana. Prana radiates from the sun, permeates the atmosphere and animates Mother Earth herself.

Breathing is our primary relationship with Prana. Our breath is a sacred gift. It is an exchange between the outer world and our inner world. Each inhale we take is a precious drink of life, an individuation of the eternal life force. Every exhale is a merging back into the eternal. It is a flow of the masculine and feminine, receiving and giving, a dance of body, soul and Spirit as one. It is, in essence, a perpetual celebration of being. It is the most palpable way in which we experience and interact with the Divine. Connecting with our breath on this level is itself among the highest forms of Yoga. Pranayama is thus both the practice of mastering and enhancing this life force and our most tangible connection with the Divine.

We lose our Prana in myriad ways. Agitated speech, over-talking and a constant inner dialogue with ourselves diminish our Prana. Negative emotions, anxiety, fear, anger, worry and grief drain this sacred energy. Mass media, over-exercise, poor diet and wrong lifestyle do the same. Not living the Yamas and Niyamas as best we are able also leaves us with less Prana.

The mind itself is a manifestation of Prana and is deeply impacted by the state of our pranic energy. Pranayama, therefore, is also an essential tool for bringing the mind under control so that we can enter into a peaceful, contemplative state. This elevates us spiritually as well as healing the body and mind, diminishing pain, and relaxing and invigorating us. As the fourth limb of Yoga, it also begins to set the stage for the deeper, more interior practices to come.

Sutra 2.49 *Tasmin Sati Svasa Prasvasayor Gati Vicchedah Pranayamah.*

"A firm posture being acquired, the movements of inhalation and exhalation should be controlled. This is Pranayama."

The firm posture mentioned in this Sutra is Patanjali's definition of Asana. Once we can sit with steadiness and comfort, we are ready for Pranayama, which precedes the deeper practices of withdrawing the senses, contemplation and meditation. We have balanced our lifestyle, settled our minds a bit, purified and strengthened our body through the first three limbs of the Raja Yoga system, and can now enhance our life force to further our Yogic journey.

This purification is essential. Pranayama practiced with an imbalanced body and mind can actually derange us further rather than help us to heal. While it is much more subtle than Asana, it is far more powerful and must be approached mindfully and with proper guidance.

Sutra 2.50 *Bahya Ahabyantara Stambha Vrittir Desakala Samkhyabhih Paridrsto Dirghas Suksmah.*

"The modifications of the life-breath are either external, internal or stationary. They are to be regulated by space, time and number and are either long or short."

In this simple Sutra, Pantanjali provides the foundation for all Pranayama practices, which have become extremely complex and detailed over the centuries. We breathe in, breath out, and retain the breath at the top of inhalation or bottom of exhalation, regulating it with mathematical formulas, timed sequences or spaces between the breaths. Through these techniques we not only strengthen our Prana, we vitalize the body right down to the cellular level.

The average person breathes at only about one third of their capacity. This shallowness of respiration contributes to a wide range of physical and emotional discomfort and disease. With our blood less oxygenated, our organs and tissues repair and heal more slowly. The blood transports fewer toxins to the lungs to be expelled via exhalation. Our immune systems are less able to ward off disease and bacteria. Vital systems atrophy, blockages arise, and we function at diminished capacity. This is why Pranayama is also a primary form of yogic medicine and central to self-healing.

Physiologically, the science of Pranayama is directly related to the autonomic nervous system. This system is comprised of the sympathetic and parasympathetic nervous systems. The sympathetic system, with nerve cell clusters along the spinal column that connect to nerve centers throughout the body, helps regulate the function of our respiratory, immune, endocrine, digestive and reproductive systems. In real and perceived emergencies, it pumps adrenaline into the system from the adrenal glands and blood sugar from the liver. We have come to know this as the "fight or flight" response.

The parasympathetic nervous system, which runs down from the brain stem, controls the functions of the internal organs and the sensory fibers that inform the central nervous system about our well being. The two systems are somewhat opposite, yet complimentary rather than antagonistic. Following the fight or flight response, once the mind perceives that the emergency has subsided, the parasympathetic system takes charge to re-harmonize and rebalance the body and mind, bringing them back into homeostasis.

Our breath mirrors and reveals these opposite functions. When we are agitated, frightened, angry or feel threatened, the breath becomes short, choppy and forced. When we feel relaxed and at peace, the breath is deeper, smoother and calmer. In our modern world, stress and anxiety have become the norm. As a result, our sympathetic nervous system is overactive and our breathing is shallow and agitated. We are filled with adrenaline, ever on guard in fight or flight mode. Given this chronic tension, the parasympathetic system has little chance to step in and recalibrate us.

Most of us do not know how to relax, which involves truly being with ourselves in the present moment. Instead, we substitute distractions as artificial forms of relaxation. We drink alcohol, watch TV, go shopping, surf the Internet, talk on the phone, click on the radio, play sports, jog or work out. The athletic pursuits, of course, are the healthiest of these choices and can exhaust us into relaxation and help release tension, but none of these pursuits gives the parasympathetic system the cue it needs to take over and retune our operating systems.

Deep breathing immediately sends us this message. It tells us there is no longer a predator at the mouth of the cave, that everything is okay, that we can let down our guard and truly relax. When active or agitated, our mind is in the beta state, which when charted on a graph appears spiky and choppy. When relaxed, the mind produces alpha waves, which are more flowing, smooth and even. All true healing is based upon this relaxation, as are all true spiritual practices. Pranayama facilitates our entering into the alpha state.

When an animal is wounded, it intuitively enters this state. It crawls into its cave, or some similar safe haven, and licks it wounds. It holds still, stops doing, and completely lets go. We have largely forgotten this essential instinct. As a result, with all the stress and fast pace of our lives, we are perpetually "walking wounded." Even our medical system, which typically seeks to medicate us with sedatives and anti-depressants, only provides a distraction, a masking of the symptoms that creates an illusion of relief. True relief, however, is always available to us, embodied in the power of our breath.

Yoga holds that there are 72,000 pranic channels in the body, called *Nadis,* which distribute Prana throughout our being. It is important to remember that Prana is both our primal life force and consciousness itself. The three most important Nadis are named *Ida, Pingala* and *Sushumna.*

Ida and Pingala nadis are associated, respectively, with lunar (feminine) and solar (masculine) energies. Both flow up from the root chakra, *Muladhara,* at the base of the spine. They cross around the higher chakras and are associated with the left (Ida) and right (Pingala) air passageways of the nostrils. Typically, one of the nostrils is dominant during our daily breathing, alternating every 90 minutes or so.

The single most important Pranayama practice, called *Nadishodana* or alternate nostril breathing, seeks to balance these breaths and their respective energies. Ida is associated with the left nostril and right hemisphere of the brain. Pingala corresponds with the right nostril and left hemisphere of the brain. By balancing these nadis we balance our active and passive states of mind. This unites Shiva and Shakti, or cosmic potency and cosmic consciousness. Over time, with sustained practice, this allows the Sushumna nadi to open. This is the most important nadi, running from Muladhara to *Sahashara*, the crown chakra at the top of our heads. When open, one is said to be in a state of enlightenment, with a peaceful mind, inner clarity and the liberation of true Self-realization.

There are five primary aspects of Prana, called the Prana Vayus, which are also energized and mastered through Pranayama and other Yogic practices. They are:

Udana:	Ascending Prana
Prana:	Inward moving Prana
Samana:	Equalizing Prana
Vyana:	Diffusive Prana
Apana:	Downward moving Prana

These aspects of Prana becomes very scientific and complex, linking these Vayus to organs and specific areas of the body, physical functions such as speech, digestion, elimination and reproduction, and various subtle functions of the mind. Udana is said to provide our capacity for sustained effort, Prana energizes us, Samana provides nutrition, Vyana governs circulation and Apana facilitates elimination. In advanced practice and therapeutic situations, we can work with each Vayu through specific Pranayama techniques, but it is enough for most practitioners to sustain an awareness of, and connection to, the breath through deep breathing and other basic techniques.

Sutra 2.51 *Bahyabhyantara Visayaksepi Caturthah.*

"There is a fourth type of Pranayama that occurs during concentration on an internal or external object."

Patanjali notes that beyond inhalation, exhalation and breath retention (at the top of the inhale or bottom of the exhale), a fourth aspect of Pranayama naturally arises as a result of yogic practice. This is when our concentration and awareness become focused enough that the breath naturally slows and periodically stops. This stillness of the breath, called *Kevala Kumbhaka*, is a sign of a still mind, and occurs quite naturally in true meditation.

Sutra 2.52 *Tatah Ksiyate Prakasavaranam.*

"As its result, the veil over the inner light is destroyed."

This reaffirms the very definition of Yoga, which Patanjali notes at the outset of the Sutras, that Yoga is a stilling of the fluctuations of the mind so that we can connect with the Soul. Since the mind arises from Prana, the practice of Pranayama is essential to Yoga.

The very essence of this inner light, or Soul, is love. Prana arises from love and love transmits the greatest Prana. This is why love heals. Babies suffer and can even die if deprived of loving touch. Elderly people in successful relationships live longer and enjoy better mental and physical health. Love is the light of the Divine, embodied in our Prana, which energizes and sustains compassion, acceptance, healing and wholeness.

As a foreign correspondent in the 1980s I was in the mountains of Afghanistan with the indigenous freedom fighters who eventually expelled the mighty Soviet Army from their country. The war created the greatest refugee crisis of modern history, with 5 million Afghans, one third of the total population, forced into squalid camps along the borders of Pakistan and Iran. Many arrived in these camps severely wounded from bomb attacks, land mines and shrapnel.

In makeshift hospitals on the Pakistan border I witnessed scores of men, women and children with missing limbs, horrid third degree burns covering their bodies, and faces blinded by shrapnel. Despite this massive suffering and the lack of modern medical care, there seemed to be a profound sense of hope and purpose within each and every wounded Afghan. The Pakistani doctor in charge told me that he had never witnessed anything like it. Many of these victims, he said, managed to overcome wounds that normally would have led to their deaths. Further, he noted, Pakistanis who had been inside Afghanistan to fight the Soviets had far greater difficulties in overcoming similar injuries.

As we were filming this interview, I remembered that every wounded Afghan in that refugee hospital had a friend or relative sitting at their bedside virtually 24 hours per day. They prayed for them, touched them with compassion, helped them in every way they could. I now realize that this was the difference between life and death. The Pakistanis, mostly mercenaries, had no one by their side. They, as the doctor noted, usually died. The Afghans, provided with the Prana of love, usually survived.

Practice

Our breath comes from Spirit and departs with it. True yogic breathing must carry the intention of merging with the Divine, it cannot be solely mathematical or mechanical. It needn't be overly complicated or esoteric. It's true power unfolds with consistent and devoted practice over a sustained period of time.

Here are some techniques most anyone can practice. However, if you have high blood pressure, cardiovascular issues or other serious health problems, you should always consult a competent teacher before embarking on a Pranayama routine.

Abdominal Breathing: Lie down on your back, placing a bolster under your knees to release any pressure on your lower back.

Place both hands on your abdomen, one on the lower portion, the other on the upper portion.

Begin to breathe deeply (always through the nose) into your abdomen, feeling it expand into your hands. At the bottom of each out-breath, gently press into your abdomen to facilitate a complete exhalation.

Practice this abdominal breathing for five minutes each day, eventually working up to ten minutes.

Three Part Yogic Breathing: Start in a comfortable seated posture, preferably on the floor with crossed legs, or on a chair with the spine upright.

Begin by breathing (always through the nose) into your abdomen, as in the practice above.

After five breaths, breathe into the abdomen and then up into the ribs, exhaling from the ribs down through the abdomen.

After five breaths, breathe into the abdomen, ribs and then fully up into the chest. Exhale chest, ribs, belly, slightly contracting the abdominal muscles at the bottom of your exhale.

Practice this full, three part breath for five minutes, working up to ten.

You can also practice this breathing throughout your day as you go about regular activities. This grows awareness and mastery of the breath, plus promotes deep relaxation while energizing you at the same time.

Alternate Nostril Breathing (Nadishodana): Begin seated in a comfortable, cross-legged position or on a chair. Have your spine erect and face straight forward.

Bring the back of your left hand to your left knee. Fold the first two fingers of your right hand down into your palm. You will use your right thumb and ring finger to alternately close your nostrils.

Inhale through both nostrils, then close your right nostril with your thumb (pressing on the side of the nostril) and exhale out the left. Inhale left, close the left nostril with your ring finger and exhale right.

Alternate this way, always changing sides after you have completed inhaling.

Do ten full rounds (breathing out left/in left, out right/in right is one full round).

Equalized Breathing (Sama Vritti): Begin seated in a comfortable posture as noted above.

Breathe in slowly (always through the nose) to a comfortable count (4-6 seconds).

Exhale to the same count, so that the in-breath and out-breath are equal.

Breathe this way for two minutes then begin to hold the breath at the top of your inhale for half the count of your breathing (2-3 seconds).

After one minute begin to hold the breath out after exhaling for the same half-length of the hold on the in-breath. This becomes a ratio of 2.1.2.1.

After one minute, lengthen the holds so that they are equal to your breaths (1.1.1.1).

Breathe in Sama Vritti for one more minute.

Note: If you have any health issues, especially with your blood pressure or cardiovascular system, consult a seasoned Pranayama teacher before engaging in these practices.

*If we fail to resist
the incessant and conflicting
messages of mass media
and our fractured culture,
we surrender our consciousness
to advertisers and propagandists
whose goals are to
program our thoughts and behaviors
for their economic and political advantage.*

CHAPTER SIXTEEN
Pratyahara

Most of us are doing all the time. We keep lists of things to do, adding activities so often that our list never expires. When we are doing one thing, we are furiously thinking about all the other things we want to do. We endlessly antici-pate what is next without giving our full attention to the task at hand. We can no longer relax or hold still, much less slow the spin of our minds. Our lives have become frantic, erratic and fragmented. We have forgotten how to be Human Be-ings and instead have become Human Doings.

Thousands of years ago the sages of Yoga knew this was a problem. That was long before mass media, television, ra-dio, computers, video games, cell phones, shopping malls, automobiles and the endless distractions and indulgences that characterize modern culture! From the moment we awaken each day, which is when most Americans turn on the television, our senses are bombarded with urgent suggestions about things to do, buy, worry about, obtain, enjoy or avoid. It is no wonder that so many of our children are diagnosed with Attention Deficit Disorder. We all have it!

The fifth limb of Yoga, *Pratyahara*, is the antidote for our chronic doing and agitated minds, and in our hectic times is perhaps the most important of the eight limbs.

Sutra 2.54 *Sva Visayasamprayoge Citta Svarupanukara Ivendriyanam Pratyaharah.*

"Withdrawing the senses, mind and consciousness from contact with external objects, and then drawing the senses inwards towards the seer, is pratyahara."

Sutra 2.55 **Tatah Parama Vasyateindriyanam.**

"Then follows supreme mastery over the senses."

"Prati" means against or away. "Ahara" means food, but specifically in this context refers to the impressions and experiences we take from the external world and ingest into our consciousness. Pratyahara, therefore, means withdrawing our senses and exerting mindfulness and mastery over what we choose to take in. As we discussed in the previous chapter, building and sustaining our Prana is essential for healing and wellness. Pratyahara allows us to internalize and contain this vital energy, which is dispersed and depleted by too much external stimuli. Without an internalized consciousness we cannot meditate, we cannot truly enter the present moment, we cannot be in touch with the Divine.

The mind and body are governed by the same cosmic laws. If we eat junk food or gorge ourselves, our bodies suffer and function well below their capacity. If we take in junk impressions, which is what mass media continually offers us, or seek too many external experiences, the mind suffers and functions well below its capacity. The anxiety which most of us feel pervading the background of our lives is a direct result of too much externalization of our consciousness and the ingestion of toxic impressions. We live in a predominantly artificial environment, filled with an unnatural level of distraction and noise.

Just as a proper physical diet (which is a form of Pratyahara) fortifies the body, boosts the immune system and allows us to resist pathogens and toxins, a proper mental diet builds strength of mind, allowing us to resist the negative and toxic sensory influences that pervade our environment. If we fail to resist the incessant and conflicting messages of mass media and our fractured culture, we surrender our consciousness to advertisers and propagandists whose goals are to program our thoughts and behaviors for their economic and political advantage. In doing this, we lose control of our minds, and therefore our lives.

Whatever we hold in our minds has a deep and profound impact on our entire being, right down to the cellular level. Negative, aggressive, fearful and violent impressions have a deeply deleterious effect on the physical body, just as positive thoughts and impressions facilitate healing and balance. Since thoughts govern our actions, we eventually mirror our inner dialogue in the way in which we interact with the world around us. For instance, violent outbursts of temper damage brain cells, inject poisonous neurochemicals into the blood stream, shock the nervous system, drain Prana, reduce immune functions and promote aging. Fear and anxiety, which are commonplace, keep us in the "fight or flight" response and do similar damage, especially when they become chronic. Reducing our exposure to these impressions through withdrawal of the senses and cultivation of positive emotions promotes the production of healing neurochemicals, aids cellular repair, enhances immune function and slows the aging process.

Our associations are as important as the impressions we absorb. We tend to become like those with whom we spend our time. This is a tribal instinct designed to minimize conflict and foster harmony. If you are from the East Coast and you spend a year in the South, you will come away with a twang in your voice. The Southerner who spends their year on the East Coast will also pick up some of the eastern accent, often without even realizing it. We all get a twang from one another, a movement towards the center of the tribal way of speaking, thinking and doing.

If we listen to hateful speech and negative opinions on talk radio, or spend our time with angry, fearful, overly dramatic or self-centered people, we tend to absorb those qualities and express them to some degree. Patanjali cautions us to avoid these associations, advising that we instead spend our time with balanced and truly happy people, seek to be with our teachers and others who inspire us, avoiding the unhappy and the wicked. This does not mean to disdain or condemn others. It is essential to have compassion for them, as the Sutras also note, but this compassion does not include allowing them an ongoing role in our lives.

The mind is deeply impacted by everything it sees, tastes, touches, hears and smells. If we surrender to our senses and external stimuli we spend our lives being pulled here and there, ever looking for new sensory delights. This is the central message of the Bhagavad-Gita, in which the warrior Arjuna despairs on the eve of a great and historic battle. In this great spiritual text, Arjuna laments that he cannot slay his enemies. Those enemies are metaphors for our negative habits, impulses and desires. Krishna, acting as his charioteer, is the Divine. He rebukes Arjuna for allowing his five senses, symbolized by the wild steeds of his Chariot, to set his course. Ultimately, Arjuna surrenders and asks Krishna to take the reins and guide him to victory in overcoming his lower self.

We find elements of Pratyahara in the Yamas and Niyamas. For example, contentment, purity, non-harming, self-inquiry and constant awareness of the Divine all support Pratyahara and, in turn, are supported by Pratyahara. There is an element of withdrawing the senses in Asana and Pranayama. When we enter a challenging pose, we must focus to hold our balance, accept the stretch or sustain our strength. Bringing awareness to the breath for Pranayama also draws our attention to the interior realm and aids in calming the senses.

Speech is an essential element of Pratyahara. We are awash in sound, and speaking is our greatest addiction. Over-speaking is the primary way in which our Prana is diminished. It sustains and further deranges our busy minds, removes us from the present moment and true reality, and diminishes our ability to cultivate awareness. This does not mean that we must be mute and cut off communication with the world around us. It means we should be mindful of when we speak and what we say. We should eliminate gossip, idle talk and melodramas expressed through our words. We should seek to be authentic with our verbal expressions, speaking more from our hearts whenever possible. We should also seek times of silence, which allows us to better perceive the true world around us.

Words have incredible power. All advertising is based upon a sustained repetition of phrases that eventually permeate to the core of our subconscious and come to control our behavior. We all know the lasting sting of harsh words when we have engaged in heated arguments. Critical, untrue and vulgar words have a toxic dissonance that impact us down to the cellular level. Likewise, soothing, positive and loving words are nurturing and healing. Mantra is an effective tool in this respect and aids in stilling the mind while supporting the practice of Pratyahara.

Pratyahara contributes to balancing our Doshas, and helps bring us from the Gunas of Tamas and Rajas into Sattva. The Gunas are the three qualities, or attributes, of life. Unlike the Doshas, which are horizontal (one Dosha is not superior or inferior to another), the Gunas are vertical. Tamas is at the bottom, Rajas in the middle, and Sattva at the top. Each of us possesses all three qualities and they tend to fluctuate throughout our lives. In the spiritual practice of Yoga and the healing techniques of Ayurveda, however, moving into Sattva is essential.

Tamas is darkness and inertia, that part of us that resists change and is overly self-indulgent. Rajas is active and restless, that aspect of ourselves that helps us push forward. Rajas is necessary for overcoming Tamas and accomplishing our goals, but too much Rajas creates chronic doing, tension and force. Sattva is balance and peace in both body and mind. In Sattva we release the ego, settle the mind, enhance our inner awareness and enter into harmony with our world. Without Pratyahara, Sattva cannot be sustained.

Withdrawing our senses is also perhaps the most potent medicine of our age. When we allow ourselves to be controlled and manipulated by external stimuli we become trapped in the bubble of social conditioning. This runs so deeply that most of us do not even realize we are in the bubble. We are unaware that most of the thoughts we have day in and day out have been created for us and are not truly our own. We cannot identify the cause of our tension, stress and anxiety, much less find a way to truly end it. Pratyahara is the needle that allows us to pierce through this bubble and ultimately extract ourselves from illusion.

In addition to removing ourselves from the control of external influences, impressions and suggestions, the mind must also be purified and enriched. Mantra aids in this, as does the practice of *Pratipaksha Bhavana*, the cultivation of opposite and positive emotions. Instead of focusing on our worries, desires, fears and dramas, Yoga invites us to culti-vate positive emotions. These include acceptance, gratitude, contentment, forgiveness, peace and loving kindness. Such cultivation further enables us to release the ego and embrace the larger picture. This should be a part of our ritualized practice and done on a daily basis. It has taken each of us years to create and sustain our negative attitudes and out-looks. It likewise takes time to overcome these deep-seated mental tendencies and truly establish a new, more positive view of our existence and the world around us.

Practice

There are myriad ways to practice Pratyahara and culti-vate a more positive and peaceful awareness. Choose a few from the two lists below and slowly integrate them into your life, seeing what they have to offer you. Also, notice how your practice of the Yamas and Niyamas is supported and deepened through withdrawal of the senses.

Reduce:
• Exposure to mass media (TV, radio, Internet)
• Noisy, hectic environments
• Association with negative people

- Excessive speech and negative speech
- Reading mindless periodicals and novels
- Trips to the shopping mall
- Unnecessary telephone conversations
- Activities that tend to over-activate your mind

Embrace:
- More time in nature
- Periods of stillness and silence
- Positive thoughts of gratitude
- Self affirmations
- Awareness of your breath
- Asana classes
- Massages
- Time for reflection and contemplation

*True reality
can only be found in "the now."
It does not exist in our thought stream,
in the past or future,
in our hypothetical conversations,
self-talk,
distractions or chronic doings.
As long as we fail to fully live
in the present moment
we fail to experience true reality.*

CHAPTER SEVENTEEN
Dharana

The first four limbs of Patanjali's Ashtanga System—Yamas, Niyamas, Asana and Pranayama—are considered the "outer limbs," or external practices of Yoga. The fifth limb, Pratyahara, begins the transition to the "inner limbs" of Yoga. These inner limbs, *Dharana, Dhyana* and *Samadhi*, are known as *Samyama*, the pathway to the true light of knowledge. This inner awareness, and comprehension of our oneness with the Divine, is the ultimate experience of Yoga.

Through moral precepts and personal observances (Yama and Niyama), we begin to master our behavior, aligning ourselves with universal law, tapping into our inner power for personal transformation and shifting our awareness from a constricted, ego-based perspective to an inclusive, spiritually based view of existence. Through Asana we begin to master the body, building our strength and flexibility while expanding our limits. Through Pranayama we begin to master and enhance our vital life force, purifying the body even further and deepening our self-awareness. Through Pratyahara we begin to master the mind, extracting ourselves from the bubble of our social conditioning and moving closer to our souls.

Now comes the sixth limb of Dharana, through which we fully step into the journey of self-awareness and discovery of who we truly are.

Sutra 3.1 *Desabandhas Cittasya Dharana.*

"Dharana is the binding of the mind to one place, object or idea."

Remember at the very beginning of the Sutras when Patanjali tells us that Yoga is stilling the fluctuations of the mind so that we can abide in our true nature? Dharana is the key to this process. The mind, as has often been said, is like a monkey jumping erratically from one thing to the next. Our hectic, fast-paced culture has given all of us "monkey mind," which is why we must withdraw from it via Pratyahara in order to liberate ourselves from excessive stimuli and begin to settle the turbulence. Dharana seeks to tame the monkey, which is a challenging task.

If we do not exercise, our bodies become weak, flaccid and less capable of functioning at their full capacity. We then become more susceptible to discomfort and disease and less able to accomplish our goals. The mind is the same. Without cultivating the power of our attention, the mind becomes weaker and operates at diminished capacity. It becomes more susceptible to external influences, suggestions and observations. We lose our will power and, along with it, our ability to stay focused upon our intentions and resolves. This, too, leads to great discomfort and disease. Much of our anxiety and depression is based upon our inability to make mindful choices and then carry them out on a sustained basis.

Dharana is essential for achieving our goals. Every great scientist, artist, athlete and entrepreneur has a high level of mastery over his or her power of attention. They are able to stay focused and bring the fullness of their intelligence and Prana to the task at hand. If their five senses or the constant din of mass media easily distracted them, their ability to perform at peak levels would be greatly reduced. The results of their efforts would be mediocre instead of noteworthy. They would no longer be icons of success and examples of human potential.

When we fail to exercise our power of attention our minds inevitably wander. This causes imbalance and unrest. Mass media and entertainment quickly step in to provide us distraction and temporary relief. This results in us further surrendering our consciousness, thus deepening our befuddlement. Without these over-stimulating distractions, to which we quickly become addicted, we become bored and eventually depressed. All that our medical system offers us is anti-depressant medication, which further clouds our consciousness. So we seek more and more distraction, lost in a spiral of increasing self-indulgence and escape. Our minds become ever more fragmented and our power of attention all but dissolves. We spend our days with endless thoughts, mostly fragmented and disjointed, and are far from realizing our capacity for excellence in all that we do.

The greatest tragedy is that we begin doing the very same thing to our children before their minds have even fully formed. We stick them in front of the television, entice them with movies, give them videogames and take them to theme parks with loud music, bright colors and endless distractions. We encourage them to become enthralled with external stimuli and equate happiness and satisfaction with these experiences. As a result, most of our children are unable to appreciate the subtlety and serenity of nature or give their full attention in the classroom. As they mature, they find that they do not know themselves, and the pain of this disconnect leads many to excessive alcohol consumption, drugs and anti-social behaviors.

Power of attention is also essential for living in the present moment. We walk through most of our days paying only partial attention to our experiences. We ever anticipate the next experience. Once we enter into the next experience, however, we pay minimal attention to it as we are already dreaming about what's next. We are, therefore, perpetually "in our heads," and as a result we miss the present moment. True reality can only be found in "the now." It does not exist in our thought stream, in the past or future, in our hypothetical conversations, self-talk, distractions or chronic doings. As long as we fail to fully live in the present moment we fail to experience true reality. Divorced from reality, we cannot come to know our true selves or the nature of the Divine, much less heal or find contentment and inner peace.

To end this "monkey mind" syndrome that contributes so greatly to our suffering we must exercise our minds as diligently as we must exercise our bodies to tone our muscles. This is far more challenging, however, since there is little in our culture to support or sustain such exercise, not even in our education system. Such exercise requires us to take charge of what enters our minds and then learn to be the true creators of our thoughts rather than having them created for us. This is done through self-inquiry, visualization, mantra, spiritual study and concentration. This does not mean concentrating on an intense form of distraction, such as a video game, which only further deranges the mind and ultimately makes true concentration more difficult.

The Vedantic view of the mind offers us greater insight into the value of concentration and its importance for Self-realization. Our primary experience of the world comes through our five senses of sight, sound, taste, touch and smell. When we live in the state of the Kleshas, which is from our egos, we are caught in our aversions and attractions. It is through this ego-based lens, called *Ahamkara,* that we view, judge and process sensory input in our outer "rational" mind, or *Manas*. These reactions are filed away in our subconscious, or *Chitta*, where we remember what we enjoy and what causes a sense of pain. These memories inform our future judgments and actions, creating our patterns of behavior and forming our habits. This is the essence of social conditioning.

Behind Manas and Chitta lies our deeper mind, called *Buddhi*. This is the repository of our intuitive intelligence, our inherent inner knowing and ability to discern truth from falsehood. There have likely been times in your life when you chose a course of action that your outer mind felt was the easiest and most beneficial despite an inner feeling that your choice was not in your best interest. Not following that deeper instinct inevitably proved to be a mistake and left you with regrets. Similarly, when we engage in dishonest, toxic, selfish or destructive behavior there is always a part of us, deeper within our awareness, which tells us we are on the wrong course. We actually watch ourselves do something that our truer self knows we should not be doing, but we can never fool that deeper part of ourselves no matter what story our ego offers as a rationalization or justification. This dissonance causes our self-esteem to suffer and diminishes our integrity, leaving us weak and unable to control our lives.

Pratyahara and Dharana help us break this cycle of being controlled by sensory input and external circumstances. Single-pointed concentration helps us listen to Buddhi, which is the whisper of our Soul, and focus on our inner wisdom. It allows us to see the truth of what is, and then to chart a wiser and more mindful course in our lives. It is essential to embodying the Yamas and Niyamas and sustaining our commitment to them. Listening to Buddhi on more than an intermittent plane is the process of connecting with ourselves, of coming to understand who we truly are and aligning our lives with this wisdom.

Since stilling the fluctuations of the mind is the goal of Yoga, one might wonder if concentration is simply more exercising of the mind and therefore inconsistent with this goal. This is why Patanjali advises us to go in stages, one step at a time. We cannot still the mind without first bringing it under our control. To exert this control we must first stop the constant stimulation, reduce the input to our sensory organs, transcend habitual responses and then regain control of our thoughts and cultivate the power of attention. In an oft-used analogy, it is like a lake whose turbulent surface must subside before we can see to its bottom. Another apt comparison would be the difference between generally diffused light and the power of a laser beam.

Behind Buddhi, the Vedic model tells us, dwells the very Soul itself. This Soul is our portion of the Eternal Soul, our drop of consciousness that comes from the eternal sea of Consciousness. This is where the journey is designed to take us, and why Yoga holds that each and every one of us has unlimited intelligence, power and potential. Just as every acorn possesses the wisdom to become a mighty oak, each of us embodies the wisdom of the Divine. Tapping into this wisdom through the power of attention is how the great sages downloaded the cosmic intelligence that allowed the Vedas to come to be.

Practice

As with Pratyahara, there are many ways to practice Dharana. Below are some of the more time-tested methods. It is always best to pick a primary practice and stay with it over a sustained period of time. However, several of these techniques can be integrated into your Sadhana, and each has great value. Dharana should always be practiced seated and not lying down. When beginning your practice, always remind yourself of *Vidya*, that you are an eternal being and embodiment of the Divine. Do not over-exert yourself or exert great effort, as this is counterproductive. Ease into Dharana and allow it to unfold.

Tratak: Tratak is the process of bringing single-pointed concentration to the mind via the eyes. A candle flame provides one of the most time-tested and effective objects for this practice.

Begin seated, either cross-legged or on a chair. Have a lighted candle at eye level, just 2-3 feet from your gaze. As you stare at the flame, do your best not to blink. Hold your awareness firmly on the flame, without wavering, for 2-3 minutes.

Then, close your eyes and follow the image of the flame in the darkness behind your eyelids. It may move, change colors, expand, contract or even disappear and reappear. Just follow whatever you see with your inner gaze for 2-3 minutes.

Softly open your eyes and gaze again at the actual flame for 2 more minutes. Notice its various parts: the blue cone at the base, the white cone at the tip, its overall shape, and the glow that arises and expands from the center of the flame.

Finally, close your eyes one more time and follow the inner image once more for a final minute or so. When you end the practice, notice the quality of your mind and the level of your awareness.

Mantra Japa: Repeating a mantra, which is called *Japa*, is like a Yoga pose for the mind. In this practice, it is traditional to use *Malas*. Malas are strings of 108 beads, usually separated by a knot between each bead, designed to help us count the number of repetitions of Mantra Japa. Each time the mantra is repeated, one moves to the next bead until an entire round has been completed. If you do not have a mala, they are easily obtained via the Internet or at many Yoga studios. But a mala isn't required, and you can still practice Mantra Japa and simply time yourself.

There are many mantras from which to choose, and it is often best to consult a Vedic teacher for a personal mantra. If you do not have a mantra, Patanjali recommends OM as the ultimate mantra, which is a good place to begin.

Begin with one round of mala beads, or with 2-3 minutes of repetition. Slowly increase your practice to 3-5 rounds or 5-10 minutes.

Breath Japa: This is a similar practice to Mantra Japa, using mantra without mala beads and adding greater focus on the breath.

Again, there are again many mantras one can use in this practice. Among them are *So Ham* (pronounced hum), which basically means "I Am," and mirrors the sound of the inhale and exhale; *OM Shanti,* for peace; and *OM Namo,* for "I Bow (to the light within me)."

Take a seated posture, with the spine erect and eyes closed. Connect with the rise and fall of your breath, allowing it to be smooth and even. Silently repeat your chosen mantra, harmonizing it with the flow of your breath. For instance, breathe OM on your in-breath, Shanti on the out-breath.

Practice for 2-3 minutes in the beginning, working up to 5-10.

Chakra Dharana: One can also focus attention on a chakra, or energy vortex, in the body as a form of concentration. Patanjali mentions the heart center, *Anahata Chakra*, and the eyebrow center, *Ajna Chakra.*

The heart center, right behind the breastbone in the center of the chest (not the organ of the heart itself), is the repository of our positive emotions such as peace, love and compassion. The eyebrow center is the seat of the mind and our higher intelligence. Lower chakras are not recommended for this practice.

As with the above practices, take a comfortable seat, close the eyes and bring your awareness to your chosen chakra. Maintain this awareness for 2-3 minutes, working up to 5-10. This practice can be deepened by breathing into and out from the heart or eyebrow center. Let the breath be effortless during this practice.

We are not the body,
the mind, the breath
nor the many roles we assume in our lives.
We are not our nationality,
our gender,
nor our religious or political affiliations.
We are not consumers,
constituents or even citizens.

CHAPTER EIGHTEEN
Dhyana

While meditation arises from consistent and devoted practice, meditation itself is a state of consciousness far beyond practice that we eventually experience as a result of our sustained and consistent efforts. In a true state of meditation, our thoughts, emotions and desires subside, and we become liberated from our turbulent minds. We enter into a state of awareness through which we merge with our object of contemplation or concentration in Dharana. This means we truly have come into the present moment, which is the only place where authentic consciousness resides. It is in this state alone that we can make contact with our Soul and come to understand who we truly are.

Meditation, called *Dhyana* in Sanskrit, is the seventh limb of Patanjali's system. As you recall, the sixth limb of Dharana, or single-pointed concentration, is the binding of the mind to one place, object or idea. In Dhyana, we go deeper and fully merge with the focal point of our concentration.

Sutra 3.2 *Tatra Pratyayaikatanata Dhyanam.*

"Dhyana is the continuous flow of cognition towards that object."

Most of us spend our days fluctuating between fear, anger, disappointment, frustration, anxiety, sadness, happiness, anticipation and so forth. All of these shifting emotions, and the memory of the impressions and sensory experiences that created them, tend to bubble up when we enter into stillness and silence. This is much like being outdoors in nature and not hearing the buzz of the insects or call of the birds until we have settled down and relaxed both body and mind. When we practice meditation, the inner turbulence of our mind is amplified and we often feel discomfort, especially in the beginning stages.

This again reveals the wisdom of Patanjali's system, in which he first asks us to embrace right living and right thinking, purify our bodies and minds, energize our vital life force and concentrate our minds before meditation is approached. Otherwise, we actually run the risk of deepening our imbalances and neuroses. A businessman who cheats his clients five days per week cannot simply show up each Sunday for an hour of church and expect that his life is an example of faith, morality and goodness. Similarly, we cannot live imbalanced lives, eat wrong foods, think toxic thoughts, get caught up in our dramas and live through our egos and expect to merge with the Divine during meditation, even if we sit for a full hour every morning and evening.

Still, practicing meditation or attempting to concentrate can have profoundly positive effects even for novices and imbalanced practitioners. As our turbid minds begin to settle after a period of sustained practice over time, we enter into a state of authentic relaxation. In this state we switch from the sympathetic nervous system, with its "fight or flight" response, to the parasympathetic system, that recalibrates us and promotes inner harmony. As noted earlier, this is where true healing begins. Western medicine has begun to realize this, as clinical studies have shown meditation is often stronger medicine for serious illnesses than medications and other conventional allopathic modalities.

But the ultimate goal of meditation is far beyond relaxation and healing. It is to experience who we truly are and live according to this wisdom. We are not the body, the mind, the breath nor the many roles we assume in our lives. We are not our nationality, our gender, nor our religious or political affiliations. We are not consumers, constituents or even citizens. We are pure consciousness, embodiments of the Divine, one with the eternal being, whom we variously call God, Allah, Ishvara, Yahweh or simply our higher power. We are *Atman*, the Soul or true Self, an individuation of *Paramatman*, the Eternal Soul. This realization is the goal of the highest form of Vedantic meditation, called *Atma-Vichara*.

Atma-Vichara basically means self-inquiry or, more appropriately, Self-inquiry, since we are looking beyond our smaller sense of self and ego and realizing our true, higher Self. This is the very essence of the Yoga Sutras and of Yoga itself. In this state of cognizance we move past our petty concerns, release our judgments and get over our attachments. We are fully out of the bubble of our social conditioning and fully in the eternal stream of the never-ending present moment. We experience our oneness with Spirit and the eternal aspect of existence. We realize our true relationship with Mother Earth, understanding that we are one with her and that our physical being arises from her five elements of earth, water, fire, air and space. We truly open our heart centers and merge with the Divine.

This is a state of awareness that we must eventually carry into our lives far beyond our Yoga mats or meditation cushions. This does not mean that we walk around disconnected from society, dreamlike and ethereal, passive and withdrawn.

It means we live with greater truth, clarity, perception and focus. Once we are free of our smaller self, we are liberated and empowered to manifest our most creative, authentic and potent Self. We understand the grace in being present, even during the most tedious and insignificant of tasks. As the ancient Buddhist saying goes, *"Before enlightenment, chop wood and carry water. After enlightenment, chop wood and carry water."*

The Sutras offer us many other focal points for our concentration and meditation. These include meditating on the heart center, eyebrow center, the sound of OM and following our breath. Then, in an embodiment of the very essence of Vedantic spirituality, which is fluid and open rather than dogmatic and restricted, Patanjali offers this option:

Sutra 1.39 *Yathabhimata Dhyanad Va.*

"Or by meditating on anything one chooses that is elevating."

This very simple and open sutra is deep and liberating. It empowers us to find what resonates for us rather than dictating exactly what we must do or not do. Yoga and Vedic wisdom are spiritual practices, but not religious practices. They are not dogmatic and exclusive, they make no spurious claim that those who do not subscribe to a rigid ideology are wrong and condemned to some sort of hell. One can meditate upon Buddha or Christ, Krishna or Shiva, Kali or the Virgin Mary.

This Sutra does caution us to make certain that our choice is elevating. Remember, in true meditation we merge with the object of our focus. If our choice of focus is at all toxic, self-centered, imbalanced or inappropriate, we do ourselves great harm. There are New Age proponents who advocate meditating on our material desires so that we might, for example, manifest a new home more easily. This is a perversion of the practice and only serves to strengthen the ego and our lust for material possessions.

It is true that universal energy is attracted to the objects of our thoughts, intentions and desires. This is why hypochondriacs have more illnesses than persons confident about their health and wellbeing. There is great power and potential in setting goals and staying focused upon them. Yoga supports this process and assists us in taking skillful action towards realizing our goals. However, these goals should be peaceful, selfless and mindful rather than self-indulgent, wistful and purely materialistic. Rather than meditate on any goals, we should focus on enhancing our inner awareness and divinity. We can then revise and pursue our intentions with greater energy, balance, wisdom and integrity.

Vichara inquiry plays an essential role in determining the quality of these choices. Through self-inquiry we can watch our thoughts and explore any situation to determine if we are being driven by the ego and the mind. If so, we should detach from our intentions and reconsider our course of action. If, however, we realize that our motivation arises from the Soul, we should seek to manifest it with vigor, determination and complete commitment. This is also the process of releasing our karma.

Karma is the inevitable experiences we will have as a result of our past actions. As the Bible warns, whatever we sow, so shall we reap. When we act from the ego, we create vast webs and knots of karma in our lives that eventually bring suffering. We release this process and truly transform our lives when we base our actions on the wisdom that arises from our Souls. To access this intelligence, we must meditate upon the very nature of being, establish true dialogue with our highest Self, and then – most importantly – act in accordance with this inner guidance.

This process of Vichara is the ultimate expression of human existence. The culmination of all embodiments is to be embodied as human form because we humans have freedom of choice and consciousness. Plants and animals live naturally in their Dharma, without choice or contemplation. We alone are gifted with the ability to ponder and choose. This allows us to chart our own destiny, but it also allows us to choose misery. We can perpetually seek to fulfill our lower desires and indulge ourselves in myriad ways, or we can access the very best within us and choose fulfillment. The Soul within us never suffers. It is eternal and pure. The body and mind suffer or thrive based upon our choices and subsequent actions. Every choice we make determines our destiny, be it misery or bliss. This is the law of karma from which none escape.

The highest form of meditation, therefore, is not those techniques that only still our minds, relax our bodies and reduce our stress, despite how beneficial these experiences might be. The highest form is to recognize our Souls. The extent to which our Soul goes unrecognized during our lives determines the level of our suffering. We must use meditation to get clarity on our *vasanas*, or collection of intentions, habit patterns, desires, attitudes and future actions. We must determine which are serving our higher purpose and which are dragging us down. We must then continuously strive to show up as our best Selves, to access our greatness and support it in every way possible. This requires strengthening our intellects, or Buddhis, and cultivating true discrimination and right action. We must look through our fears, doubts and indecisions, shine sacred light on our inner darkness and truly come to know our authentic Self. The more we access and listen to this inner voice, the more we move deeper into our truth. Once we are seated in our Souls, our lives move towards grace, humility, compassion, fearlessness and joy. We seek to serve others, honor all of life and always stand in the truth of Yoga. This allows our Dharma, or true calling in life, to unfold and blossom. This is liberation. This is the promise of Yoga.

Practice

There are numerous meditative techniques in Yoga, and each of us must find what works best for us according to our temperament and level of awareness. In a general sense, however, there are two main approaches. One is passive mindfulness and the other is active inquiry. Passive mindfulness practices include observing our thoughts, following our breath, systematic body awareness, cultivating detachment, watching a river flow by, gazing at the sky or contemplating a deity or cosmic principle. These practices are experiential, but there is no discernment or direct practical application to our daily lives. Nevertheless, these are important, powerful and useful techniques for healing, moving us forward, refining our perception of reality and bringing us into the present moment.

Active inquiry, which is a higher form of practice, is like a sharp sword that cuts through our illusions. It is the very process of discovering the Self. It connects us with eternal wisdom and compels us to analyze our behaviors and perceptions and then make appropriate changes over time. Yet we should not necessarily choose to bypass mindfulness and jump right to Atman-Vichara and active techniques. We must truly assess where we are in our journey, take one step at a time and have patience. It is always advised to seek guidance from a seasoned teacher who is more likely to have a clearer view of where we are in our journey than we might have ourselves.

Passive Mindfulness Meditation

The techniques of Mantra Japa, Tratak and Chakra Dharana detailed in the Practice section of the last chapter are all capable of leading you into meditation. Your practice of Dharana, when sustained over time, will result in a merging with the object of your concentration.

You may also choose to simply follow the breath, hold your awareness at the heart or eyebrow center, contemplate your chosen deity or watch your thoughts.

In any of these techniques, begin seated, either cross-legged or on a chair. Ensure you are in a quiet place where you will not be distracted or interrupted. You might begin with five minutes of meditation and slowly build up to longer sittings. It is more important to practice daily rather than try to do lengthy meditations that you are unable to sustain on a regular basis.

To strengthen your commitment to your practice and enrich your experience, find a small place in your home that
you can devote to your practice. Make it sacred by creating
an altar. It can be as simple as a candle and a few beautiful
stones or as elaborate as you like. Each time you sit, begin by lighting your candles and perhaps some incense. Pay
homage to Mother Earth, the Spirit that dwells within you,
and to the Divine in whatever form resonates for you. Then,
embrace your meditation as the centerpiece of your spiritual
practice. If you have an already established Asana practice,
it is best to do it first, followed by some Pranayama, and then
your Dhyana.

Most importantly, choose one technique and stay with
it for many months or even years. Constantly seeking new
practices or switching between various techniques merely
provides a distraction and diminishes our experience.

Active Inquiry Meditation

The Eight Limbs of Yoga themselves are each a form of
Vichara Meditation. In focusing on the Yamas and Niyamas,
and seeking to align our lives with these precepts, we enter into
a form of inquiry and contemplation. True Asana practice
includes connecting more deeply with the body and the Prana
of each pose. Pranayama itself connects us with our vital life
force. Through Pratyahara we inquire as to how our senses
work and the manner in which external forces influence us.
Dharana, of course, is the gateway to Dhyana. Samadhi, the
final limb, is the ultimate result of our practice.

In Vichara, we can inquire into one of the limbs of Yoga,
who we really are, the nature of the Divine, our Prana,

Mother Earth and her five elements or our Karma. There are many more choices, but the ultimate Vichara is into the Atman – our Soul. Such contemplation should be practiced as noted above in the mindfulness meditation section.

*When we embrace
what we formerly perceived as sorrows,
our misery dissolves
and is replaced with grace.
We see behind the surface
of superficial reality,
perceiving the deeper,
more eternal truth
of each and every circumstance.*

CHAPTER NINETEEN
Samadhi

It is possible to live much of the rest of your life free from suffering, stress, anxiety, worry, anger and uncertainty. You can cease reacting to the ups and downs of the world around you and become content, experiencing profound joy and fulfillment in every moment, feeling connected, grounded and whole. It is even possible to be so fully merged with cosmic reality that you perceive the Divine in all things and the oneness of all that is. This is *Samadhi*, the eighth and final limb of Patanjali's system.

Just as the sustained concentration of Dharana leads to the meditative state of Dhyana, sustained Dhyana leads us to Samadhi, which translates as absorption. In this state of immersion we are freed from the Kleshas of our ego, likes, dislikes, judgments and fears. We live fully in the present moment, and each action we take is sacred and mindful. Washing and cutting vegetables for dinner, or doing mundane errands, is as blissful as a vacation or sunny day at the beach.

In Samadhi, we are always connected with our higher Self, we have full potency, complete balance and pure potential. This is *Satchitananda,* or Being (Sat), Consciousness (Chit) and Bliss (Ananda). We are in radiant mental and physical health, out of the bubble and established in our true nature. Most importantly, our spiritual suffering, born of the ego, is eradicated. We have transcended our lust for material goods and sensory indulgences. We are no longer estranged from our hearts, no longer in sorrow, no longer incomplete or lacking anything.

This is the pinnacle of Samyama: the tri-fold practice of Dharana, Dhyana and Samadhi. It is a state of super-consciousness in which we remain fully conscious and functioning in our world but are no longer its pawn or victim. It is a surrender of our smaller self, an embodiment of Yoga, an end to our karmas, vasanas and obstacles. The great scholar and mythologist, Joseph Campbell, puts it beautifully with this observation:

"We're in a free fall into the future. We don't know where we're going. Things are changing so fast. And always when you're going through a long tunnel, anxiety comes along. But all you have to do to transform your hell into a paradise is to turn your fall into a voluntary act. It's a very interesting shift of perspective... Joyfully participate in the sorrows of the world and everything changes."

This is the essence of being in this world but not of it. It is a surrender of our desperate desire to control all outcomes and an acceptance of all that is. It is an understanding of our true position in the universe. When we embrace what we formerly perceived as sorrows, our misery dissolves and is replaced with grace. We see behind the surface of superficial reality, perceiving the deeper, more eternal truth of each and every circumstance. It is not only recognizing that a higher power than our individual self is at the helm, but actually turning our lives over to that higher power and accepting the course that is charted.

This is what the great warrior Arjuna finally did in the Bhagavad-Gita. As you recall, he despaired on the battlefield of his life as he faced his darker side, and was rebuked by Krishna (a symbol or archetype of the Divine) to see past his ego and petty concerns, release desire, fear and self-centeredness, and to stand in Yoga and fight his battle to victory. When he finally got the message and his doubts dissolved, Arjuna surrendered to Krishna, effectively giving him the reigns of his chariot and acknowledging the wisdom of allowing his higher power to set the course.

Sutra 3.3 *Tad Evarthamatra Nirbhasam Svarupa Sunyam Iva Samadhih.*

"Samadhi is the same meditation when there is the shining of the object alone, as if devoid of form."

This means that we move beyond our meditation and become fully absorbed in the object of our contemplation. In other words, we become one with it. Patanjali goes on to say this brings the true light of knowledge. It is this knowledge, which now has become wisdom, that allows the truth to fully unfold. All delusion is dissolved. We have a "cosmic clarity" through which we can be ultimately perceptive, skillful and creative. He further tells us that this state brings enormous powers, including knowledge of the past and future, our past lives, the mental state of others, complete control of the senses, plus great strength, insight, awareness and even supernatural powers. Yet he cautions that these powers are not the goal and should not be fixated upon. Eternal peace through oneness with the Divine is the ultimate resting place of our journey.

It can be said that there are lesser and false Samadhis. At its root, Samadhi is complete absorption. When we become fully absorbed, even for a brief time, we feel relieved of our suffering and sorrow. False Samadhis that provide this relief are at the base of our addictions. Alcohol, drugs, gambling, pornography, chronic shopping, television, video games and other forms of mindless entertainment to which we surrender our attention are all false Samadhis. In effect, they are delusional forms of contentment that allow us to escape ourselves yet, at the same time, enter into a sense of the present moment which typically escapes us.

Lesser Samadhis, which are legitimately uplifting and not necessarily destructive, include stepping beyond our perceived limit into great adventure, such as climbing a mountaintop, the "runner's high," and the absorption into complete intimacy in the arms of our beloved. We take vacations in search of lesser Samadhis, hoping to escape all of our obligations and worries and truly relax and let go. Great thinkers, like Einstein, are said to have arrived at their greatest insights and theories through the process of Samyama: concentration, meditation and Samadhi. They have accessed a form of the very same cosmic wisdom that the composers of the Vedas downloaded during their Samyama thousands of years ago.

Living in true Samadhi on a sustained basis is elusive, and something very few of us can ever expect to achieve. Those who do are our saints and sages, our Krishnas, Christs and Buddhas. It is wondrous enough for most of us to have glimpses of this higher state of awareness, and to continue moving towards it and seeking to sustain it more fully in our lives as best as we are able. The more we experience this state, the more genuine and authentic we become, and the less the loops, hooks and knots of our habituated lives hold sway. As we release more of our smaller selves and open to our true nature, we move towards becoming *Jivanmuktis*, or liberated beings.

Self-realization and self-liberation go hand in hand. Once we realize who we truly are, we are on the road to liberation from the tyranny of our conditioning and circumstance. Even without being in a constant state of Samadhi, we can extract ourselves from our past habits and patterns, we can free ourselves from the bubble of social conditioning and see it for the illusion it is; we can open our hearts and interact with the world as sacred, loving, peaceful, joyous and humble beings.

Not only is this the essence of transformation, it is utterly revolutionary. We are no longer merely puppets in a commercial system of enterprise, statistics for the Consumer Price Index, or consumers of the endless and predominantly worthless offerings of a money-based capitalist economic and political system. We have unlocked the shackles of our individual ego and the collective ego of our culture, and released ourselves from one of the most subtle, insidious and effective systems of human control, manipulation and brainwashing ever created. This is our birth right as Divine Beings.

The final sutra Patanjali gives us speaks of **Kaivalya**, or independence, absoluteness and liberation. This supreme state, he continues, arises from **Chitisakteh**, the power of pure consciousness. Yoga is, thus, the sacred, universal science of developing human potential and furthering human empowerment. It brings us into the present moment, face to face with the highest reality, and equips us with the tools and techniques for true spiritual awakening and personal growth. Although it was divined millennia ago, it has never been so relevant, necessary and vital as it is today to heal us and make us whole on both an individual and collective basis.

While we mere mortals might not slip into eternal Samadhi and complete enlightenment as a result of a single lifetime of Yoga practice, each and every one of us has an amazing potential and phenomenal power to transform our lives for the better and to manifest our fullest potential. In doing so, we make a significant contribution to the furthering of humankind, as well as ourselves. Patanjali has provided us a clear and detailed map for the journey. All we need do is take one breath and one step at a time, with sustained practice and detachment as to the outcome, remaining stable, focused, committed and disciplined.

At the same time, we must keep our hearts open and treat ourselves with understanding, forgiveness, compassion and acceptance, realizing that true and lasting change does not come overnight, or even in weeks or months. We will surely stumble, occasionally fall back, disappoint ourselves and make mistakes. This is part of the human experience. But never lose faith and never forget that you are capable, powerful, sacred, beautiful and Divine. May you ever live fully blessed in Yoga!

*For the yogic journey
we must do our best to embrace
moral precepts and personal observations,
then acquire some mastery of the body,
breath and mind.
We can then withdraw from external stimuli,
concentrate our awareness,
connect with who we truly are
and ultimately
find lasting liberation.*

CHAPTER TWENTY
Deep Yoga

The profound intelligence embodied in the Yoga Sutras provides us a roadmap for our journey, guiding us into personal transformation and Self-realization. In our teaching school, Deep Yoga, we seek to reach as deeply as we are able into the depths of this wisdom and apply its relevance to our modern lives. We are further guided and informed by Ayurveda and its holistic system of healing, natural balance and wellness.

The Deep Yoga name is also derived from the Sanskrit word, *Dipa*, pronounced "dee-pah," which is the lamp of the Soul mentioned in the Bhagavad-Gita when Krishna discusses shining the light of wisdom on the darkness of our ignorance. This does not mean ignorance as an insult. It refers instead to the human condition of being seated in our egos, forgetting who we truly are and therefore suffering. Deep Yoga is designed to bring practitioners back into their hearts, realigning them with their inherent power and Divinity.

In Deep Yoga Asana-based classes, we approach practice as a spiritual exercise. We apply the Kriya technique of the Sutras, harmonizing body, breath and mind through Asana, Pranayama and Pratyahara. Silent mantras such OM Namo (which we use to mean "I bow to the light of consciousness within me") or OM Shanti (a mantra to peace within and without) are used as Yoga poses for the mind. These inner mantras then lead and move the breath, which should be deep and full, slow and smooth. The breath, in turn, leads the motion of the body and moves us into and out of our poses. This creates an inner harmony, deepens our awareness and brings us more fully into the present moment. We employ Samyama, the practices of Dharana, Dhyana and Samadhi, through using focal points for our consciousness such as the heart center. In this state of concentration and meditation, we open to compassion, gratitude, acceptance and lovingkindness. Ultimately, we merge with the object of our concentration and move towards absorption and Samadhi. This does not mean that each class brings us into full Self-realization but, if we do our job well, students experience the depth of what Yoga has to offer and are inspired to move forward.

Many of the poses in Deep Yoga classes are approached as physical embodiments of Divine aspiration. When we reach high into the air it is to acknowledge and touch the Divine. A forward fold is both a folding into our heart and a bowing into Mother Earth. We invite students to surrender their egos, move past likes and dislikes, and release suffering. We invite them, as well, to embrace their inherent power, unlimited potential, beauty and grace. We weave in various Pranayamas, meditative themes and teachings from the Sutras, Bhagavad-Gita, Upanishads and other sacred texts. We also create space between poses for experiencing the Yoga of stillness and silence.

In Deep Yoga practice, the level of one's presence is far more important than the depth of one's pose. Developing our strength and balance to the point that we can finally perform a headstand or hold a Warrior Pose, or increasing our flexibility so that we can finally touch our toes in a folding posture, are all signs of devotion, dedication and progress. These advancements build our self-esteem and expand our limits, which is wonderful and should be encouraged and applauded. Ultimately, however, Yoga is the practice of merging with the Divine.

Our bodies are the temples of our Spirit. If we are expressing a very advanced pose and feeling a bit superior, we are in our egos and far from this sacred Spirit. If our fingertips seem miles away from our toes in a forward fold, but we have released our ego and are harmonized with our breath and inner mantra, immersed in the light of our hearts and fully in the present moment, we are much more in a true state of Yoga and the accomplishment of touching our toes is secondary.

Creating and sustaining a home practice is another essential component of Deep Yoga. This can be fairly simple and short, designed to complement the schedules and demands of your busy life rather than add another stress or strain. Your practice should be approached from an Ayurvedic standpoint of balancing your Dosha. The simple test in the Appendix of this book can help you determine your Dosha, or individual constitution.

If you are predominantly Vata, which is associated with the element of air, you want to focus on poses that ground you, plus cultivate stillness and strength. If you are predominantly Pitta, which is associated with the element of fire, you want to focus on poses that relax you, plus cultivate inner peace and surrender of the ego. If you are predominantly Kapha, associated with the element of water, you want to focus on more active poses, plus cultivate motivation and discipline. It is always beneficial to consult a seasoned teacher for further guidance in this regard.

As you begin your home practice, take a few moments in stillness and silence. If you have an altar, which is highly recommended, light a few candles and remind yourself that you are a Divine Being, and that your practice is ultimately one of unfolding your highest Self and connecting with Spirit. Do your Asanas next, always using an inner mantra to guide your breath, and your breath to guide your body.

The most important poses you will practice are the cross-legged seated posture as you begin and the *Savasana*, or relaxation posture at the end. Follow Savasana with Pranayama, which should also be done with advice and guidance. End with concentration or meditation. Once you have completed your practice, remind yourself again of the sacredness of your practice and bow into the light of your heart.

It is even more important that we seek to bring Yoga into our lives as fully as we are able. The Yamas and Niyamas guide us in this effort, and Ayurveda supports us with proper lifestyle practices. Self-transformation involves changing our lives in small and sometimes great ways. We cannot think ourselves into positive change, nor can we find lasting change through external means. It is challenging work. It takes great devotion and consistent practice. We must face our shortcomings, confront our demons and move forward with tremendous conviction and faith. We should not delude ourselves into believing we can quickly attain Samadhi or Self-realization and bypass aspects of practice that we find challenging. This is the very essence of Tapas, or self-discipline and sustained effort.

Patanjali offers us a step-by-step process to unfold Yoga in our lives. It is analogous to building a house. We must first lay a foundation, then construct a frame, adding plumbing and wiring in appropriate sequences, moving from stage to stage until completion. Only then do we have stability, integrity and something we can call a home.

For the yogic journey we must do our best to embrace moral precepts and personal observations, then acquire some mastery of the body, breath and mind. We can then withdraw from external stimuli, concentrate our awareness, connect with who we truly are and ultimately find lasting liberation. We are then Jivanmuktis, or liberated beings, still living in this world but not of it, no longer perceiving through the ego or reacting when things fail to go according to our self-centered script, but instead acting skillfully—contributing, mindful, advancing humankind.

The hard work is worth it. It is the greatest investment you will ever make. Inner peace and advancing humanity in our own humble way are both priceless. Ultimately, Deep Yoga is an invitation to return home to your heart, to live from your greatness, to be present in each and every day as the amazing being that you truly are. May you ever be blessed to live in Yoga and shine your light upon all that is!

*The journey
of Self-transformation
and spiritual awakening
takes great courage.
First, we must face ourselves
and acknowledge
the circumstances we have created
which have caused our suffering.
We must then resolve to take action
and change these circumstances.*

CHAPTER TWENTY ONE
Sutra Tools

Most humans have an inherent fear of change, even when we have habits and behaviors that we know are not in our best interest. We spend much of our lives creating and sustaining our life patterns. They eventually form the borders of our comfort zones and define who we are. This creates a great inner resistance to anything outside this zone. It is almost as if our habits have a mind of their own that vigorously argues with us, and even seeks to subvert our efforts.

The journey of Self-transformation and spiritual awakening takes great courage. First, we must face ourselves and acknowledge the circumstances we have created which have caused our suffering. We must then resolve to take action and change these circumstances. This takes hard work, and must be sustained and nourished each and every day.

Beyond the Eight Limbs of Yoga, Patanjali's Sutras offer us a variety of tools and techniques to aid us on our journey. Several of them have already been mentioned. In this chapter, we highlight many of these aids with suggestions on how to apply them to your life.

Sthira & Sukkha: Sthira and Sukkha, or steadiness and comfort, are central to yogic practice. Seek to find your center and be grounded, stable and strong in both your practice and all that you do to improve yourself. At the same time, don't force it. Find sweetness and comfort despite the challenge of your efforts. Force inevitably creates resistance and constriction. Inner peace, no matter how difficult the circumstance, promotes ease, clarity and skill in action.

Pratipaksha Bhavana: Pratipaksha Bhavana, or cultivation of opposite and uplifting emotions, provides a magic key to free us from habitual negativity, anger, fear and defensiveness. Through cultivation of gratitude, acceptance, compassion and peace, we can slowly shift our view of the world around us. We should practice cultivating these positive attitudes as often as possible, even when we are not bogged down with dark feelings. The more we do this, the more we move into harmony, balance and grace.

Abhyasa & Vairagya: Abhasya & Vairagya, or practice and detachment, help remove the ego from our efforts and keep us from being overly anxious about if and when the benefits of our efforts will appear. We should practice for practice's sake, remaining detached from the shifting circumstances around us while letting go of our desires, aversions and attractions. The benefits will appear when they appear, and even when we reach a goal we should continue to sustain our efforts.

Prasadanam: We retain our Prasadanam, or undisturbed calmness, through cultivating attitudes of friendliness towards the happy, delight towards the virtuous, and disregard for the wicked. This means that we should seek the company of those with positive attitudes and those who are on a journey similar to ours. We should spend time with our teachers and others who inspire us. We should remove ourselves from the presence of negative people and those whose lives are imbalanced and toxic.

Sraddha, Virya, Smriti & Prajna: Through Sraddha, or faith, we reaffirm our belief in our inner power and our connection with the Divine. We release any negative self-talk and disregard any naysayer around us. Through Virya, or courage, we move forward with great conviction and determination, knowing that while we might stumble or fall now and then we can overcome all obstacles, and nothing can stop us from manifesting our intentions. Through Smriti, or the power of memory and retention, we can hold onto what we have experienced and learned, accessing this wisdom whenever we need. Through Prajna, or flashes of insight, we can connect with our Soul and learn to follow its guidance.

The Kleshas: Virtually every difficult situation we find ourselves in, and every negative reaction of ours we wish we had not had, can be traced to the Kleshas of Avidya (forgetting we are Divine), Asmita (identification with the ego), Raga (attraction), Dvesa (aversion) and Abhinivesa (fear). Through cultivating a constant awareness of how the Kleshas impact our lives, we can ultimately move past them and return to natural wisdom. Whenever you find yourself in fear or anger, walk yourself through the Kleshas and notice how they define your circumstance. Then trace your way back to remembering who you truly are.

Deep Yoga

ARE YOU VATA, PITTA, KAPHA?

DETERMINING YOUR DOSHA IS KEY TO ACHIEVING YOUR OPTIMAL HEALTH, WELLNESS, SERENITY, & SUCCESS.

Doshas:

VATA

Vatas tend to be creative, imaginative and sensitive. When Vata is out of balance, anxiety and other nervous disorders may be present. Digestive problems, constipation, cramps, and even premenstrual pain usually are attributed to a Vata imbalance.

PITTA

Pitta people tend to be intelligent with a sharp wit and a good ability to concentrate. Fire is a characteristic of Pitta, whether it shows up as fiery red hair or a short temper. Toxic emotions such as jealousy, intolerance, and hatred should be avoided to keep Pitta in balance.

KAPHA

Kaphas are strong, calm and steady with a positive outlook about life, but, when out of balance, can become stubborn and lazy. Kaphas need stimulation to bring out their vitality.

YOUR DOSHA ~

Please check any that apply and total them below each section:

Physical	Temperament	Under Stress
Thin frame____	Talks fast or a lot____	Loses weight____
Prominent joints____	Indecisive____	Constipation____
Very tall or short____	Learns fast, but forgets____	Excess gas____
Variable appetite____	Enthusiastic/joyful____	Restless/active____
Weight at middle____	Psychic____	Chronic pain____
Chilly____	Sensitive to noise/lights____	Light sleeper____
Dry kinky hair____	Creative/artistic____	Anxious/fearful____
Small dry eyes____	Intuitive____	Variable energy____
Joint discomfort____	Introspective____	Panic attacks____

TOTAL____

Physical	Temperament	Under Stress
Medium build____	Words sharp/concise____	Rashes____
Athletic____	Competitive____	Excess sweat____
Warm blooded____	Intelligent/perceptive____	Body odor____
Oily, soft skin____	Keen memory____	Gastritis/ulcers____
Freckles/pimples____	Irritable/impatient____	High blood pressure____
Premature gray____	Successful____	Sleep sound/short____
Straight fine hair____	Jealous____	Eats hot spices____
Pink, pliable nails____	Courageous____	Alcohol to excess____
Undue hunger____	Organized/efficient____	Anger/violent temper____

TOTAL____

Physical	Temperament	Under Stress
Thick, wide frame____	Slow speech____	Over sleep____
Good stamina____	Calm____	Overeat/ or loss
Strong____	Responsible____	Of appetite____
Thick oily cool skin____	Steady faith____	Excess mucus____
Weight in hips/thighs____	Slow memory/but prolonged____	Water retention____
White, even teeth____	Stubborn____	Overweight____
Thick lustrous hair____	Forgiving____	Lazy/inert____
Large eyes____	Loyal____	Greedy____
Well lubricated joints____	Nurturing____	Depressed____

TOTAL____

Deep Yoga: www.deepyoga.com

GLOSSARY

Abhinivesa: Fear, ultimately the fear of death. The fifth and final Klesha.

Abhyasa: Steadiness; practice.

Ahamkara: The ego.

Ahimsa: Non-harming, the central moral precept, or Yama, of Yoga.

Ajna Chakra: Chakra at the eyebrow center.

Anahata Chakra: Chakra at the heart center.

Anumana: Inference.

Apana: Downward moving Prana, one of the five Prana Vayus.

Aparigraha: Non-possessiveness.

Aptopadesha: Instruction.

Asana: Yoga posture.

Ashtanga: Eight Limbs of Yoga as outlined in the Yoga Sutras of Patanjali.

Asmita: Identification with the ego, the second of the five Kleshas.

Asteya: Non-stealing, one of the Yamas, or moral precepts of Patanjali's Ashtanga Yoga system.

Atman: The true Self.

Atma-Vichara: Meditation of inquiry as to the nature of the true Self.

Avidya: Lack of wisdom, the first of the five Kleshas.

Ayurveda: The holistic healing system that is the sister science of Yoga.

Bhagavad-Gita: A sacred text of Yoga.

Bramacharya: Abstinence, one of the Yamas or moral precepts of Patanjali's Ashtanga Yoga system.

Brimhana: Tonification. Process of strengthening.

Buddhi: The higher, rational aspect of the mind.

Chitta: The subconscious aspect of the mind.

Dharana: Single-pointed concentration, the sixth limb of Patanjali's Ashtanga Yoga system.

Dharma: Universal, eternal law. In a personal sense, Dharma is one's true path in life.

Dhyana: Meditation, the seventh limb of Patanjali's Ashtanga Yoga system.

Dipa: The lamp of the Soul.

Dosha: Mind/body types of Ayurveda: Vata, Pitta and Kapha.

Dukkha: Suffering, anxiety.

Dvesa: Aversion, one of the five Kleshas.

Gunas: Fundamental attributes of nature, Tamas, Rajas and Sattva, as used in Ayurveda.

Hatha Yoga: Yoga practices focusing on physical purification as a preparation for Raja Yoga.

Hatha Yoga Pradipika: Seminal text of Hatha Yoga, written by Swama Swatmarama in the 15th Century.

Ishvara: The Divine, God.

Ishvara Pranidhana: Costant awareness of the Divine, one of the Niyamas of Patanjali's Ashtanga Yoga system.

Japa: Repetition, typically of a mantra.

Jivanmukti: Liberated being.

Kaivalya: Independence, absoluteness and liberation.

Kapalabhati: A Pranayama and purification technique involving powerful and quick inhalation and exhalation through the nose, often translated as "skull-shining."

Kapha: One of the three Doshas, associated with water element.

Karma: The inevitable results of one's prior actions.

Karma Yoga: The Yoga of Action in which one performs one's duties without regard for the outcome. Karma Yoga often involves selfless service to others.

Kleshas: Afflictions, or causes of suffering.

Krishna: Incarnation of Vishnu and central deity in the Bhagavad-Gita.

Langhana: Purification technique of "reducing" through fasting.

Mahabharata: Spiritual epic of India that contains the Bhagavad-Gita.

Mala: String of 108 beads used in Mantra Japa and meditation.

Manas: The externalized aspect of the mind.

Moksha: Liberation. Literally, "aloneness."

Muladhara Chakra: Chakra at the root or tailbone area of the body.

Nadis: Energy channels of the body.

Nadishodana: Alternate nostril breathing in Pranayama.

Nidra: Yogic sleep, a state of mind without any perception.

Niyamas: Personal observances. The second of the eight limbs of Patanjali's Ashtanga Yoga system.

Ojas: Fluid of life. One of the three Vital Essences.

OM: The ultimate mantra, the sound of the Divine, also sometimes written as AUM.

Paramatman: The ultimate, eternal Soul.

Patanjali: Ancient sage and composer of the Yoga Sutras.

Pitta: One of the three Doshas, associated with fire element.

Prajna: Flash of Divine insight.

Prakriti: The basic matter of which the universe consists.

Pramana: Right knowledge.

Prana: Vital life force, also one of the five Prana Vayus (Pran), and one of the three Vital Essences.

Prana Vayus: Five aspects of Prana.

Pranayama: Yogic practice of mastering the breath and energizing the life force, the fourth limb of Patanjali's Ashtanga Yoga system.

Prasadanam: Undisturbed calmness.

Pratipaksha Bhavana: Cultivation of opposite, positive emotions.

Pratyahara: Withdrawal of the senses, the fifth limb of Ashtanga Yoga.

Pratyaksha: Direct perception.

Purusha: The cosmic, eternal self.

Raga: Attraction, one of the five Kleshas.

Rajas: Action, turbidity. One of the three Gunas.

Raja Yoga: The Royal Path of Yoga, also known as Patanjali's Ashtanga Yoga system.

Sadhana: One's personal, daily practice of Yoga.

Samadhi: Absorption, the eighth limb of Ashtanga Yoga.

Samana: Equalized, balanced Prana, one of the five Prana Vayus.

Samyama: Dharana, Dhyana and Samadhi, the inner three limbs of Ashtanga Yoga, known as Samyama, the pathway to the true light of knowledge.

Santosha: Contentment, one of the Niyamas of Ashtanga Yoga.

Satchitananda: Being, consciousness and bliss.

Sattva: Tranquility and balance, one of the three Gunas.

Satya: Truthfulness, one of the Yamas, or moral precepts, of Patanjali's Ashtanga Yoga system.

Satyagraha: Mahtama Gandhi's non-violent philosophy used to expel the British from India.

Saucha: Purity, one of the Niyamas, or personal observances, of Patanjali's Ashtanga Yoga system.

Savasana: Corpse Pose, the final pose of relaxation in Yoga Asana practice.

Seva: Selfless service to others.

Shanti: Peace.

Shukra: Reproductive tissue and fluid.

Smriti: Memory.

Sraddha: Faith.

Sthira: Steadiness.

Sukkha: Comfort.

Sushumna: Central energetic channel, or Nadi, of the body.

Svadhyaya: Self-inquiry, one of the Niyamas of Patanjali's Ashtanga Yoga system.

Tamas: Darkness and inertia, one of the three Gunas.

Tapas: Self-discipline in spiritual and transformational practice. One of the Niyamas, or personal observances, of Patanjali's Ashtanga Yoga system.

Tejas: Inner radiance, one of the three Vital Essences.

Tratak: Concentrated gazing, such as gazing at a candle flame.

Udana: Ascending Prana, one of the five Prana Vayus.

Upanishads: Hindu scriptures central to Vedantic wisdom.

Vairagya: Detachment.

Vasanas: Collection of intentions, habit patterns, desires, attitudes and future actions.

Vata: One of the three Doshas, associated with air element.

Vedanta: India's spiritual tradition of Self-realization that arises from the Vedas.

Vedas: The most ancient spiritual texts of India.

Vichara: Inquiry.

Vikalpa: Imagination, wishful thinking with no basis in fact.

Viparyaya: False knowledge, involves delusion, illusion or hallucination.

Virya: Courage.

Vyana: Diffusive Prana, one of the five Prana Vayus.

Yamas: Moral precepts, one of the eight limbs of Patanjali's Ashtanga Yoga system.

Yoga Sutras: Sacred text on Yoga written by the sage Patanjali.